M000297649

PRAISE *for* BETHANY, GOD, & ME

"Can someone really find hope amid heartbreak, especially when that heartbreak is the pain of losing a child? Thankfully, the answer is a resounding yes.

I highly recommend my dear friend's book *Bethany, God, and Me.* With great courage, vulnerability and humility, Bonnie Bolander tells the story no parent should ever have to experience. Once she embraces that God uses everything in life to bring His children closer to Him, she has one of the most tragically beautiful moments with God I have ever read. I couldn't stop the tears. This is a story that will stick with you long after you close the book."

MELODY BOX, Author of *He Can Be Trusted:*
Discovering God's Presence in Your Darkest Moments

"This book serves as an encouraging reminder that God's grace and hope are interwoven with the pain we often experience. As Bonnie shares her story, she gives us an inside look at the pathway of growth that God laid specifically for her in the midst of a life-altering time. In doing so, she courageously teaches us that pain can serve a greater purpose when we allow it to be used as a tool of refinement in our lives. This book proves that "beauty from ashes" is not something reserved for biblical times, but rather, it's a narrative that a loving God is still writing for His children."

COURTNEY BOLANDER, President, Radiant Hope, Inc.

"*Bethany, God, and Me* is a beautifully transparent look at a mother's journey through her daughter's struggles and destructive choices. Bonnie Bolander pushes back the social taboos to expose the deep heart issues that accompany the topic of suicide. Her willingness to divulge her own battles with perfection will speak to parents at any stage, from newborn to adult children. Her determination to hold on to what she knows is true is a great reminder that God's steadfast love and faithfulness is evident even in the darkest moments. This book is a beautiful picture of choosing to live in the midst of profound grief, healing in the aftermath of deep hurt, and trusting God to use it all for His glory."

KAREN TAYNE, Family Minister of Preschool
MacArthur Blvd. Baptist Church

"Bonnie shares with her readers the intimate story of the love and loss of her precious daughter, Bethany. With raw honesty, she shares how the Lord watched over her during this difficult time and how she leaned on Him to get through it. The book will touch your heart and give you hope."

PEGGY HORNER, Premier Designs, Inc.

"Bonnie and Bob Bolander have been family friends for over two decades. We met through the common ministry of Lake Ann Baptist Camp. Bob was serving on the board when they called me to serve as their Director of Development. That was more than 25 years ago.

The week that Bethany chose to change all of our lives forever, two of our sons were staying at their home in Flower Mound, Texas. Our boys were there that Saturday morning.

Bonnie's journey, and the lessons she has taken from it, are important to any family member or friend who has been touched by a loved one's suicide. I pray that as you read each chapter, Bonnie's story ministers to your soul and brings you closer to the Savior.

My family was forever changed when Bethany took her life. We are forever better from watching Bonnie and Bob trust the Lord to bring beauty from ashes."

KENT WALLACE, President, Vision Works Consulting

"Bonnie has allowed herself to be transparent in this book and share what was going on in her heart as Bethany struggled with her demons. She has also conveyed the glorious truth about our loving Father and how He is sufficient to not only ease the pain of the loss, but to equip us to move forward in life on mission for Him.

I am blessed to call Bonnie a friend and sister in Christ. I love watching how she interacts with women of all ages, and speaks truth into their life situations. Serving with her on the Women's Ministry Team at MacArthur Blvd. Baptist Church allowed me to grow in my love for the Lord and get a new perspective of the needs of women.

Regardless of where you are in life, you will relate to the heartache of this story, and you will rejoice over the truth that is revealed through Christ."

LINDA PHILLIPS, Director of Women's Ministry,
MacArthur Blvd. Baptist Church

Bethany, GOD, & Me

Hope in the midst *of* heartbreak

Bonnie Bolander

BOUND BY HOPE
PUBLISHING

Bethany, God, & Me
Hope in the Mist of Heartbreak
Bound by Hope Publishing, web or contact

ISBN 978-1-7337580-0-0

Unless otherwise noted, Scripture quotations are from the New American Standard Bible® (NASB), Copyright © 1960, 1962, 1963, 1968, 1971, 1972, 1973, 1975, 1977, 1995 by The Lockman Foundation Used by permission. www.Lockman.org

Scripture quotations marked (ESV) are from the ESV® Bible (The Holy Bible, English Standard Version®), copyright © 2001 by Crossway, a publishing ministry of Good News Publishers. Used by permission. All rights reserved.

Scripture quotations marked *(The Message)* are taken from The Message. Copyright © 1993, 1994, 1995, 1996, 2000, 2001, 2002. Used by permission of NavPress Publishing Group.

Scripture quotations marked (NIV) are taken from the Holy Bible, New International Version®, NIV®. Copyright © 1973, 1978, 1984, 2011 by Biblica, Inc.™ Used by permission of Zondervan. All rights reserved worldwide. www.zondervan.com The "NIV" and "New International Version" are trademarks registered in the United States Patent and Trademark Office by Biblica, Inc.™

Cover photo © Victoria Schaad; Interior teacups © Lana for AdobeStock.com

Edited by
Tim Grissom, editor

Design by Monica Thomas for TLC Book Design,
TLCBookDesign.com

Printed in the United States of America

To my sisters

Diane, Debbie, Angela, Becky, Joy, and DeAnn
whether by birth, marriage, or in Christ.

Each of you has invited me in to be a part of your
daughter's life, a beautiful gift indeed.
I am forever grateful.

A WORD *of* THANKS

Writing a book, I have learned, is both a solitary journey and a group outing. There were so many who came alongside.

My Prayer Team

Your steadfastness to bring this project before the Father carried me to complete this task. Thank you for your faithfulness, the checking in, the words of encouragement and affirmation, and all your support. Thank you for praying for those who will read these words, for asking God to use this message to bring hope and healing to another life.

My Writing Team

Madison, thank you for typing my original manuscript. You have no idea how helpful this was to me. DeAnn, for your guidance, influence, and encouragement—thank you.

Kent and Debbie, truly, there are no words to adequately express my gratitude. You both have spent countless hours pouring over this book, listening to me, brainstorming, praying for me, and instilling confidence when I wanted to give up. Both of you have been a priceless treasure. Thank you.

My Voices of Truth

Josh, you have encouraged me for many years to finish this task, and you had the courage to tell me I really needed an editor. You were right! Thank you.

Tim, your skill, wisdom, and tenacity have been invaluable. You took what I had to offer and helped me learn to make it so much better. Thank you for your investment into this book. Your expertise, encouragement, and friendship have been a gift to me.

My Family

Parents, brothers, sisters, nieces, and nephews, you walked this road with our family. You loved us well, you gave, and you sacrificed for us. Thank you. I deeply appreciate the years of praying and encouraging me to see this project through. I am blessed to belong to such a wonderful group of people.

My Sons and Daughters-in-Love

Scotty and Ricky, God has abundantly blessed me with both of you. Thank you for never being resentful toward us for your teenage years. Thank you for your encouragement and support as we walked with Bethany in her pain. You both gave up much because of the crisis at hand. Yet, you loved—you loved us and you loved her well. Our family was broken, but not beyond repair. Thank you for being such an integral part of the healing. I'm grateful for the laughter, the love, and the friendship.

Starr and Courtney, you have both been such beautiful additions to our family. Thank you for loving our sons well. Without a doubt, it has both strengthened them and encouraged their healing. Thank you for your friendship and love. You are both gifts.

God has used this tragedy in all our lives, whether it's been to instill passion and purpose deep within, resulting in ministry around the world*, or to introduce you to your partner in love and life. I love our little family. Thank you for your encouragement and support.

My Best Friend

Bob, how could we have walked this road alone? I am grateful that God led us together on this painful journey. You are a remarkable gift. A listening ear, a voice of reason, a comforting embrace, an enabler of dreams. Thank you for the freedom you've given me to tell our story. Thank you for your commitment to me, to our family, and to our Lord. Your leadership in our home and through our trial has been a beacon of light and a source of hope. I love you.

---

* For more information, see *Radiant Hope Ministry* on page 117

Contents

FOREWORD

One of the things I enjoy the most about traveling overseas is the extended time on the plane. Strangely, I look forward to the travel more than I do the destination. I pastor a large church and I have a large family—meaning that seven hours of uninterrupted quiet is rare. I literally have to fly to the other side of the world to get that kind of time.

A few years ago, I began planning—weeks in advance—for an upcoming trip to Africa. I carefully chose the books I wanted to read, the articles and blogs I wanted to catch up on, and the books of the Bible I hoped to consume. I couldn't wait to sit down, put on my headphones, take out my books and journal, and for just a few hours, enter into a world of introverted bliss.

The week before I left, one of my favorite church members, Bonnie Bolander, handed me a large manila folder and asked if I would be willing to read something. She had just written the first three chapters of what she hoped might someday be a book. She wanted to get my thoughts on what she had done so far. I took the envelope and gladly agreed to read it. I placed it in my stack of books for my trip and took it with me to Africa.

As I sat on the plane and opened my bag to get out my first book, I made a quick decision to take out Bonnie's envelope and read her chapters first. I really don't know how to describe what happened over the next few hours. Bonnie had ruined my flight! She had not only disrupted my plans, she had disrupted me. I was unprepared for the way her story affected me. I sat in my seat with those papers in my hand, surrounded by strangers, and cried.

When I first got to know Bob and Bonnie, I learned the basic details of their story. I knew a little, but not much. Frankly, from what I did know, I didn't want to know more. I have four daughters, and the Bolanders' story was my worst nightmare. I had no real desire to think more about what I regarded as the unthinkable. But suddenly I was confronted with all that I had never wanted to know.

Through my own suffering, I have learned that in order to learn from it, you must enter into it. You must remember what you long to forget. You must meditate on what you want to ignore. You have to sit and let the pain and the questions settle in. You have to be willing for the pain to break your own heart. I realize that this is counterintuitive. Getting away from the pain as quickly as possible makes sense. This seems to be the only logical way to cope with it. But in reality, we must enter into it in order to properly navigate our way out of it.

In this book, Bonnie enters in. She opens the doors to rooms that at first feel like they should remain shut. She talks about things that we think might be left unsaid. She brings up things that seem better left alone. She enters in. And, she invites us to go with her. But...she also brings us into her healing. She shows us how God takes pain and turns it into something beautiful.

In 2013, my wife was diagnosed with stage-four cancer. She was the healthiest person I knew. The news was shocking, to say the least. After her treatment was completed and it appeared that God was restoring her health completely, I fell apart. I was an emotional, physical, and spiritual mess. And as we walked through our suffering, I learned one very important lesson: there are no exceptions. We are all broken people. Suddenly I realized that each Sunday morning I stood before a congregation of the hurting and wounded. I had never had that thought before in my life.

But sadly, most of us have not been prepared for this inevitable reality. We always seem surprised when life gets hard. We are shocked when *we* are the ones with the bad news or diagnosis, but in reality, we should know that broken people living in a broken world will have pain. And it's not only inevitable, it is a primary way in which God intends to accomplish His purposes in our life.

This is why I'm so glad Bonnie wrote this book. It's not just a story, it's a guide, showing us why we need to enter into our own suffering and how to navigate it, and reminding us of what we most often forget in our times of suffering: God knows how to take something terrible and turn it into something beautiful. This is a book about hope.

If you ever get the chance to meet Bob and Bonnie Bolander, you will certainly feel the way I felt when I first met them—you will want them to be your friends. There is a sincerity, a love, a grace, a peace, and a depth of wisdom about them that you want in your life. You will find that time with them is life-giving. And if you get to know them, you will discover that all the things you love the most about them have been born out of their most painful moments.

So, as you read this book, enter in. Not because you love suffering, but because you love what suffering produces. And as you enter in, I pray that "the God of hope [will] fill you with all joy and peace in believing, so that by the power of the Holy Spirit, you may abound in hope" (Romans 15:13, ESV).

J. Josh Smith
Sr. Pastor, Prince Avenue Baptist Church
Athens, Georgia

INTRODUCTION

This is the story of a teenage girl, a good God, and lessons He showed her mom through the girl's struggles and eventual suicide—lessons about who she was deep inside and lessons about who He is. I am that mom, and many days I wish this wasn't my story. Most of the time, though, I am grateful for the things He showed me and for His faithfulness to carry me through the pain that resurfaces even after all these years.

We all have a story to tell; some of our stories are compelling, some are tragic, and some are even mundane. Some can be told outright and proudly, others with transparency and humility. God is the one who authors them, and they are always best read within the framework of His epic design and plan.

The problem with suffering is that we rarely see it for the gift it can be. Heartache, pain, trials, and loss all have ways of revealing our true character. They also influence our view of God and the direction we will take in life.

To be honest, when our family's trial began, I thought we'd be the last people on earth to find ourselves in the specific set of circumstances we did. But since God is the author of our stories, He knows exactly what we need to be drawn closer to Him. He knows that trials have the potential to form deep, authentic relationship.

My purpose for writing my story is to demonstrate that surrender to God's work in our heart through any trial is not something to avoid or fear. Rather, because of His unfailing love and infinite goodness, we can trust Him to do a beautiful work in us—a work that will yield a bountiful harvest of blessing.

Like soil, our hearts must be prepared if they are to produce, and preparation means cultivation. The ground will be stirred and turned over, the crust will be broken, the rocks and stones removed. *Un*cultivated soil rarely yields anything but weeds. I have learned that it is to my advantage to surrender to pain and heartache, seeing beyond the immediate to the beautiful thing it can produce in me.

It is also my desire that you, the reader, would seek after God's heart, learning from Him, but also about Him, His beautiful character and His deep, deep love for you. In seeing God for who He is, we have a better chance at seeing ourselves for who we really are. There is no comparison. But in the seeing, we learn to trust Him more, even when we hurt.

My story has no power to change a heart, but I have prayed it will point you to the One who can. You may be quite familiar with many of the truths God revealed to me, but perhaps you will see them in a new light. My prayer is that you will grow as you learn to surrender your own heart for God to prepare.

As you read, you might feel some frustration over the details I've left out. You may wish to know more of the story, but I am not the only player in this tale. In an effort to love and respect my husband and two sons, I've left some things unsaid. Perhaps they will each tell their own version of this story someday, but that is up to them. As with any eyewitness accounting, there can actually be multiple versions of truth as the events impact each person differently, based on roles and relationships. I am telling my perspective and the things God has taught me through our loss.

I am eternally grateful that we are a family still intact, happy and healthy, though separated by miles. I present this book with the blessing of each family member. ૭৯

Dear Bethany,
We grieve because you are gone.
We rejoice that you are free from the cares of this world.
We are grateful that we were chosen to be your parents.
We love and miss you,
Mom and Dad

…we do not grieve as those who have no hope.
I THESSALONIANS 4:13

*People need to see
what truth looks like
on fallen, broken,
and imperfect souls.*

1

Truth Serum

"Daddy, does the pain go away when you're in heaven?"

Our sixteen-year-old daughter's question brought back the all too familiar feelings of desperation and fear. My hope for her survival was slipping away.

Bethany didn't have a terminal illness, yet her pain was as palpable and her future as uncertain as if she did. Someone had stolen her innocence and, along with it, her hopes, dreams, and the desire to live.

Ignorance Is Bliss

Bethany had first attempted suicide nineteen months earlier. We were living in Flint, Michigan, at the time. I had been in Detroit for a meeting, and as I was driving home, I called my husband to let him know my ETA. My son answered the phone.

"Hey, Scotty. Can I talk to Daddy?"

"Mom, don't freak out but..."

✦ ✦ ✦

Bethany had revealed to us earlier that fall what we had long suspected. As she had become less like her usual self and more withdrawn and isolated, we poked our parental noses where they supposedly didn't belong. We just wanted to know the truth.

For a while it had been easier not to know. There was comfort in ignorance. It wasn't peace though; it was denial. But the bliss was quickly and completely swept away by the news I received over the phone. Bethany had been rushed to the hospital. She had tried to take her life.

✦ ✦ ✦

The girl on the hospital gurney was not my daughter. *No! My daughter would never say such things. She would never do the things she said she'd done. And why was she thrashing around? Why do they have her restrained?* My mind could not wrap itself around what I was seeing and hearing.

"No, sweetie, you aren't an addict!"

What I was really saying was … you can't. You can't be these things you think you are, because you are my daughter, and my daughter wouldn't do or be these things.

I began to panic. *This can't possibly be true!* Yet here was my precious firstborn child convulsing and spewing sordid details of her recent past. It was as if she had downed a bottle of truth serum with the fist-full of pills she had taken. My ears were stinging from her confessions. She was yelling them out for the whole world to hear. With only curtains as walls, I was certain the entire hospital staff had evaluated our parenting style and had already pronounced us a dysfunctional family. They'd probably even written it on her chart. *But my husband is a pastor. Our family isn't supposed to have problems like this. What will we tell people? What will they think of us?*

> *I was in bondage to what I believed others thought of me as a parent.*
>
>

I had a twofold revelation right then and there: (1) My daughter was in more pain than I realized, and (2) I was in bondage to what I believed others thought of me as a parent. As my daughter lay there baring her soul, all I could do was bury my face.

Along with these revelations came great loss. Not only was I losing my daughter to a mind and heart filled with pain, I was losing a self-imposed expectation of a perfect life. I would soon be lightened of that load. Loss—of many kinds—would become a big part of this journey.

✦ ✦ ✦

Bethany was stabilized and transferred to the ICU. After consulting with a friend, we agreed to a sanitized version of the truth to tell our congregation the following morning. "Bethany had an adverse reaction to some medication she took."

The little band of believers at our church didn't exactly fall for our story, but neither did they judge us. They may not have known the reason, but they certainly couldn't have missed the changes in our daughter. Her once vivacious and sensitive personality had slowly slipped into coy and flirtatious behavior, and finally to sullen and withdrawn. Truth be told, they probably knew a lot more than we did.

At first Bob and I had chalked up all these changes to her age. Parents do that. We often hide our heads in the sand and think if we keep them there long enough, when we pull them out, our kids will have magically morphed into mature and responsible adults, and we can dismiss ourselves from the growing pains of the teenage years. However, our church family showed up that day and showered us with nothing but love and support. The S-word was never spoken, but they knew. They were there for Bethany, too, as well as for our sons. They talked, shared, cared; they did everything they were supposed to do. They even started a "Teddy Bear Brigade." By the end of the day, her hospital room was filled with colorful teddy bears! I know many in our little group of believers were privately suffering their own pains and tending to their own trials. But this time they had been called upon to help us. And they did.

Rude Reality

Monday morning greeted us with a transfer from the ICU in Flint to a Christian psychiatric hospital in Grand Rapids three hours away. Bob stayed home in Flint to care for the boys and made a couple of day trips over to check on Bethany and me. I went home once to check on things, but mostly spent the week between a hotel room we couldn't afford and the hospital—which we couldn't afford either. We had no medical insurance at the time, but really, who thinks of that in moments of crisis? Much of our next three years would become "act now, pay later."

In all of my denial and ignorance, I truly thought that a week in a place like this would fix Bethany and we could get back to our normal little life. Instead, during that week, she was introduced to other teens who, like her, were trying to find reprieve from their pain. She was introduced to prescription meds for her depression and a plethora of ways she could cope. Unfortunately, these helpful tips came from other patients, not from the counselors. In short, she went home armed with new ways to plan her escape into another world.

It's Over Now, Right?

We returned home, and for a couple of weeks, though constantly shadowed by fear, began to adjust to our new normal. *Surely everything's fine now, but just in case, don't talk about anything that might make her angry. Take her to school, don't ask too many questions, take her to counseling and very sweetly convince her to go in and talk.*

I would later realize that for nine months, before Bethany had revealed to us the secret behind her struggles, she had been alone in her thoughts and stewing in the words of her attacker and in the accusations of the father of lies. She had become convinced that she was bad, ugly, worthless, and shameful. Now, she was acting upon those lies.

I had great confidence in my wisdom and was absolutely sure that somehow I would be able to talk Bethany out of her feelings. If I could convince her she shouldn't feel that way, I could fix her. But I couldn't. The truth is, I had no idea what she was feeling: neither the shame that stems from being molested, nor the overwhelming desperation that would persuade her to believe that nothing but death could erase it.

Bethany knew the truth; she had personally trusted Christ and His work on the cross as the payment for her sins. His Spirit resided in her. Often I found myself frustrated that her teenage mind couldn't or wouldn't tap into the resources His Spirit offers. Even my "eloquence" could not find a way to communicate that truth to her. Every conversation I had with her up to the very last day of her life was filled with desperate pleading as well as the thought that "surely this" will cure her.

Perfection, the Grand Façade

Pride can take many forms and often stems from grand intentions. For me that meant having the desire to live a perfect life with a perfect husband and perfect children. I truly desired for people to see how good my God was, and how wonderful life can be when you live it for His glory. That trip to the emergency room taught me, though, that my heart was deceiving me (Jeremiah 17:9). I wholeheartedly desired that Christ be honored in how I lived my life and raised my children, but I was beginning to realize just how desperate I was for the approval of people around me.

> *I was beginning to realize just how desperate I was for the approval of people around me.*
>
>

The prophet Samuel learned a big lesson when he assumed who God's anointed would be. Seeking obvious qualities of importance or position to qualify for leadership, Samuel never looked beyond the externally impressive. God graciously admonished him though, "Man looks at the outward appearance, but the LORD looks at the heart" (1 Samuel 16:7). I'd been aware for quite some time of Samuel and this particular lesson God had taught him, but somehow I had missed the relevance to my own life. I thought that the best way to show others just how great God was, was to show them how perfect my life was. I thought if I did everything I was supposed to do, be as perfect as I could be, follow all the right parenting tips and guidelines, then God would certainly reward me with perfect children and a perfect life. I saw people in our church struggling with their faith, wrestling to believe that God was a good God, that all things worked together for good (Romans 8:28), so I took it upon myself to be a model of God's goodness.

> *Jesus calls us to authenticity so that He will be glorified through the transforming of our hearts.*
>
>

The idea that Christians never have problems clearly isn't found in the Scriptures at all. So why do we so often walk into the doors of our churches, pretending everything is all right, when, in fact, we may be struggling or suffering? Jesus spent much of His earthly ministry debunking this behavior. He said it wasn't the healthy that needed a physician, but the sick (Luke 5:31). He came for those in need. His kingdom would not be filled with the perfect ones, but the ones He would be perfecting; not the capable, but the ones who, through His power, would become able. As Amy Spiegel wrote, "When I fail, I am not disproving the truth of the good news, only confirming my need for a Savior."[1]

A woman approached me after hearing me share our story and how God had carried us through our pain. She said to me, "Thank you for giving me permission to be real." I gave her permission? I understand why she felt this way as I have struggled with this very thing. However, I'm not the one who gave her permission. She had it all along—from God.

Jesus calls us to authenticity so that He will be glorified through the transforming of our hearts. The Bible tells us over and over that we will suffer pain, to expect it, even to rejoice in it. If we could learn to rid ourselves of false expectations, we could be, in the words of C. J. Mahaney, "transformed by a divine perspective that [prepares us] for suffering."[2] We live in a fallen world. Pain and heartache are very much a part of this life. God doesn't necessarily receive glory when everything's perfect, although He could. God becomes very big in our eyes and to the world, however, when we, in our pain, choose to be obedient to Him and trust Him.

From Pride to Praise

The overriding lesson God would be teaching me over the next many years would be how to move from pride to praise. Pride is demanding. It stomps its feet until it gets what it wants. I wanted perfection. My heart was trying to tell me the reason was so my God would look good, but deep down I knew the truth: *I* wanted to look good.

It's difficult and humbling to walk in authenticity, but people need to see what truth looks like on fallen, broken, and imperfect souls. I heard it said that we have enough courage to share the grace and change we went through (and overcame), but we seldom have enough strength and humility to admit we need help right now. All of us struggle, most of us in silence. The truth is we're too proud to acknowledge that neither our circumstances nor we ourselves are perfect.

What do we do when we are confronted with truth? How do we respond? Will we allow the Lord of heaven, the gracious and loving God, to do His work in us? Will we be changed? That night, many years ago when my daughter took her bottle of "truth serum," God began to expose the truth of my own heart. He set me on a long journey of learning to trust Him and His plan. He began a refining process that would move me away from the pride of perfection toward the place of praise. The process continues to this day. ✺

The pride and arrogance of trying to minimize our problems and handle them in our own strength is exhausting at best and an outright failure at worst.

ᴇ 2 ᴈ

MAKING A MOLEHILL
OUT OF A MOUNTAIN

The week before Thanksgiving of 2000, Bethany joined my mom, sister, and teenage niece on a weekend cruise from California to Mexico and back. These few days drastically altered the course of her life.

She had flown out to California on her own. She was barely fourteen, and I was anxious for her to fly alone. Fortunately, I was able to connect her with a sweet older couple that would be on the same flight, and they promised to keep an eye on her. Bethany was an independent young lady, so she protested a little. But I prevailed, and she traveled safely from Detroit to Los Angeles.

Five short days later, the rest of us joined my family in California for the Thanksgiving holiday. I couldn't wait to see Bethany again and hear all about her trip. As we got off the plane, I fully expected to be knocked over by her vivacious blondness, assaulted by the many pictures I was sure she had taken. Instead, she greeted us with a long quiet hug. The long part wasn't unusual, but the quiet part was. As the rest of the family walked ahead of us toward baggage claim, I said to Bob, "Something's wrong. Something has happened to her." Bob agreed. You'd have to have known Bethany to know why it only took a matter of seconds for me to deduce this fact. She exuded life, it oozed from every fiber of her being, especially her eyes and her smile. She seldom held her feelings back. When I asked about her trip, her simple "it was fine" was a glaring clue that something had gone terribly wrong.

Our suspicions grew when we arrived at my mom's house and there were no pictures. We would later learn that Bethany had burned them.

We're Just Fine

I recall a few months later that my sister-in-law asked, "Is Bethany okay?"

"Yes, just normal teenage stuff," I responded.

What I wanted to say was, "Leave me alone! Stay out of our business! We've got everything under control! Go back to your perfect world with your perfect children!" Really, her question came from a heart of genuine love and compassion, but I just couldn't open up about our fears.

Bethany was sleeping a lot, too much. She wasn't defiant, but she was clearly carrying a heavy burden. We didn't know what to do or how to get her to talk to us about whatever was bothering her. How many different ways could we ask, "What happened on that cruise ship?" How many excuses could we make for her behavior when others inquired?

With our confusion came introspection. *Why can't things go back to the way they used to be? Why can't we get our act together like other parents do? What if Bob were more authoritative? What if I were more easygoing? What are we really dealing with? Do other teenagers sleep all the time?*

We instituted some rules: read your Bible, pray and journal every day, go to all youth group activities at the church, and join a small accountability group. Setting these boundaries put Bethany in a place to receive help and healing. Even so, though our rules weren't harsh, rules don't fix broken hearts. In the meantime, we kept asking questions, hoping we would eventually discover the right combination of words that would unlock the door to her secret pain.

We homeschooled Bethany that year. Our church was very small, so her social circle was limited mostly to the families who were in the church or part of our homeschool co-operative. She also took driver's education classes during that time and seemed to integrate herself quickly with the others. One day we received a call from the mother of a friend of a friend of a friend who wanted to let us know Bethany had been seen smoking a cigarette. *Well, thanks for that!* I thought. *Just one more thing to try to get her to admit. Why can't people just mind their own business? Are their daughters perfect? Is mine the only one who is struggling?!*

We took what would be our last family vacation that spring—to New York City. I knew the trip would be stressful, but we pushed through. A particular photograph we took still brings chills. Bob and Bethany are standing on the first level of the Statue of Liberty, and the twin towers are standing in the background just behind Bethany's head. This was April of 2001. Five months later the towers would fall. For that and other reasons, our lives would also begin to fall apart.

That summer, Bethany returned to a Christian camp in the upper peninsula of Michigan. She had attended the previous year and had enjoyed it tremendously. She had been a leader among her peers, encouraging others and growing in her walk with Jesus. It had been a spiritual high for her, and she left with a great reputation, lasting friendships, and a deeper relationship with God.

Bob had been one of the speakers the previous summer and had been asked to return. He planned to drive up a few weeks later. In the meantime, since Bethany was already at the camp, Bob wanted to surprise her by remodeling her bedroom. In the process he stumbled across her journal. Committing a parent's unpardonable sin, he began to read.

He immediately announced a change of plans: he would be leaving for camp that day and he would be going alone. After some effort, I was finally able to get him to tell me what was going on.

"Her diary," he said.

"What about her diary?"

"I read her diary."

"You what?! What did it say?"

"I want to get drunk, get high, get laid, and kill myself."

Suffering in Silence

I drove up to the camp a few days later. As soon as I stepped foot on the campgrounds I was met with a barrage of questions from concerned parents, counselors, and other teens—What's happened to Bethany? … Is Bethany all right? … Bethany's changed.

My personal favorite was, "I'm concerned about Bethany's attitude and conduct." *Oh, really? Well, join the club!* I thought. The pristine reputation she had the summer before was long gone.

I wanted to scream at the top of my lungs, "No! I don't know what's wrong! No! I do not know what happened! We are drowning here!" But I didn't scream. I didn't ask for help. I just kept making excuses, downplaying her behavior and chalking it up to being a teenager.

That week of camp ended abruptly and tragically when three college-aged members of the staff were killed in a head-on collision with a logging truck.

By nature, teenagers question many things about life. When you add trauma to the mix, life becomes chaotic. For my Bethany, God had become confusing and untrustworthy. This once tenderhearted, compassionate, and faith-filled young lady was beginning to see the world,

> *I didn't scream. I didn't ask for help. I just kept making excuses, downplaying her behavior and chalking it up to being a teenager.*

and consequently her God, through the lens of circumstances. No longer was it just her that had experienced pain, now it was several families. And in Bethany's mind, they didn't deserve the anguish.

The ten-hour drive home was solemn. None of us really knew what to say. We spent most of the drive in silence, praying for those families and contemplating the brevity of life.

The Truth Comes Out

We had a college intern working at our church that summer. On her last Sunday evening with the teens, she drove Bethany home after their meeting. They came into the house together and asked if they could talk to us. Apparently she had been brave enough to share her personal story with the girls that evening and had encouraged them to tell someone if they had experienced something similar. As a result, we finally learned from Bethany what our hearts had suspected for nine long months.

A crew member had sexually molested her on the cruise ship.

Even as she told us this horrible news, Bethany tried to downplay the assault, saying he had merely touched her inappropriately. (We would find out many more disturbing details over the next several years, confirming he had actually raped her.) She also blamed herself, saying she had told him she was fifteen years old instead of fourteen. She really believed we would be angry with her, and on top of that, she feared for her life—and ours. She was convinced that he would somehow know she had told. No amount of compelling logic on our part could soothe her. She blamed herself.

The next morning we called the cruise line to report the incident. They were not much help, but were bound by the law to report it to the FBI, who in turn set up an interview with Bethany at a local branch of the Bureau.

❖ ❖ ❖

In the meantime, Bethany began acting out upon the lies she had lived in for the past nine months, lies such as: you deserve this, you're not worthy of love, you may as well act like what you really are. We began seeing cuts on her arms, and she made excuses: the cat scratched me, I broke a frame and it cut me. The near-constant sleeping continued, her grades began to drop, and her attitude toward us and her brothers changed dramatically.

We had been awaiting a second meeting with the FBI to commence a formal investigation when that fateful morning of 9/11 rocked Bethany to her core. Her opinion of God nosedived.

So many of us in the United States were trying to make sense of this new kind of fear, this terror that had invaded our world. Finding the right words to explain to our children the "what and why" of it all was a daunting task when we ourselves didn't understand it. Searching Scripture to find encouragement, consolation, and meaning, and to bolster confidence in our God who sees, knows, and has all things in His control was challenging enough to convey to our church family but nearly impossible to convince our daughter. She was building a case against God based upon the circumstances she was witnessing and experiencing. Her actions were screaming much louder than her words, and we were forced to face our little molehill and see it for what it really was.

The Lie of Self-Sufficiency

Through this time, I had been looking at our struggle with Bethany as a molehill. Not that big of a deal really, something we could easily step over, ignore, or excuse away. Slowly, though, I began to see my self-sufficiency in a different light.

Often, we look at our circumstances and our behavior based on our limited assessment of the character of God. We may think we can handle things on our own, we don't need any help; everybody just needs to mind their own business. All the while, God sees our molehill for what it truly is: a mountain, an affront to His holy character, a subtle questioning of His wisdom, and a resistance to His unfailing love. On top of that mountain He sees a cross with His Son on it, suffering and dying for that and all sin. God knows that if we would just humble ourselves, see the mountain for what it is and come to the cross, we would also see Him for who He really is—a loving God who has remedied our every problem, including our sin, through the work of His Son, Jesus. "The power of the cross offers us redemption for our sin, reconciliation to God, removal of the wrath of God that we deserve, and a declaration of righteousness over those who have trusted Christ."[1]

The pride and arrogance of trying to minimize our problems and handle them in our own strength is exhausting at best and an outright failure at worst. The same Jesus who is the Way to God is also the Truth that allows us to see things the way they really are, to see accurately so we can deal with them effectively. Humbly recognizing our need for God on a daily and consistent basis, not trying to handle life on our own terms, leads to that abundant life that is only found in and through Jesus Christ.

I may have begun to recognize my need for God's help in all of this then, but it would be a while before I would truly surrender our trial to Him. That would be a slow and tedious tug-of-war between my pride and God's patience. I had to learn to let go. ✌

*We can collapse in shame
and condemnation,
or we can surrender
to the life-giving change.*

3

LEARNING
TO LET GO

The year of 2001 was a watershed for most Americans as the events of 9/11 ushered us into a new era of anguish. Given that, and what our family had been enduring, we hoped and prayed we would soon be able to put this awful year behind us.

Christmas was just a few weeks after Bethany's first suicide attempt, and we decided to fly to California for the holidays. In retrospect, the trip probably brought her back into her pain. We had no idea. We just needed to get away as a family.

January 2002 came in quietly. We returned home to Michigan and the kids started back to school. Things seemed to be getting back to the old normal. We had been told to keep a very close eye on Bethany as she was still considered suicidal. We tried to watch her with caution, but our denial (that things were really that bad) prevented us from seeing clearly. We hadn't given her much freedom over the holidays, either at home or in California; we did everything together as a family. So, after a week back at school with no incidents or warning signs, we allowed her to attend a weekend sporting event.

Losing Control

Monday morning was horrific. Once again my pride came under attack by a barrage of phone calls—Did you know? ... I thought you should know... How could you not know? That sickening feeling of fear, anger, and shame came flooding back over me. *How could she, and why would she, seek out the very thing that only a year ago caused her such anguish?* I simply could not wrap my head around her choices or her reasoning. I was angry and I resented Bethany for picking apart the perception of perfection I had worked so hard to establish.

One of the calls had been from the school guidance counselor. She informed me that Bethany was being suspended for fighting. This was incomprehensible. My Bethany, who had an ongoing love for all of mankind, who constantly sought out and stuck up for the underdog, the underprivileged, and the undernoticed, who never spent a day on anyone's blacklist, was being suspended for fighting? I just couldn't grasp it. And so, in deepening shame, I drove to the school to retrieve my daughter and her belongings.

Slipping Away

We barely spoke in the car. An unseen thief had come between us and had stolen the intimacy we once enjoyed. In its place was a silent awkwardness, a casual acquaintance with very little warmth or affection. We still enjoyed some precious mother-daughter moments, but they were few and far between. After this day, they would be even fewer.

Mothers anticipate and prepare for the milestones in their daughters' lives that lead to their independence. I was fully aware of that distant day when my baby girl would leave me to go off into a big world of hopes and dreams. But my heart was not at all prepared for her to sever that bind so abruptly. I wasn't done being her mommy.

I spent much of the remainder of the day on the phone with her doctor, her counselor, and family members. My sweet sister-in-law came over to be in the room with Bethany so I could have some privacy during my phone calls. Bob and I also discussed the "What's next?" question. We really had no idea what to do or where to turn.

After dinner, homework for the boys, and some family time, we were all ready to crawl into our beds to put this very long and dreadful day behind us—all of us except Bethany. She had already slept most of the day away. Bethany's room was upstairs next to ours. The daytime watch had all been downstairs; I was determined to keep an eye on her at all times. As we retired for the night, she asked if she could clean her room since she had slept most of the day. I said yes. If this meant she was moving even slightly toward a semblance of order, why would I say no?

I climbed into bed, exhausted, and began my descent into slumber when I was jolted back into reality by a large thud. I was up and at her door in a split second. She met me there, apologetic for the noise, sputtering an explanation. I accepted her word and went back to bed. But a few minutes later, she stumbled into our room like a zombie with a belt cinched tightly around her throat. She was turning blue.

In that moment, everything changed.

Our world flew into chaos. My husband at her neck, trying to remove the noose, I to the side of my thirteen-year-old son, who had stumbled onto a scene no brother should have to view. It was after midnight and all we knew was that we couldn't do this alone anymore. Who do we call? Where do we go? I asked her so many questions, as if she could come up with rational answers for her behavior. I made many phone calls, late phone calls. Grandpa and Grandma arrived, and we escorted our precious fifteen-year-old into the back of the car, armed with an adult male on either side, as I drove us to the psych ward of our city hospital. Though Flint, Michigan, didn't rank in the top ten large cities in the country, it did have the dubious distinction of being in the top five in crime. One can imagine our horror and disbelief as we handed our baby over to the attendants—who seemed more like jailers in a prison. My husband's title, credentials, or security badge wouldn't gain us any more access to her than the standard sixty minutes per week.

It took over a week to find a more suitable place for her. Before the transfer, and after nine long days, we were able to check her out for the evening to spend time with and say goodbye to Bob's entire family: two grandparents, six aunts and uncles, and nine cousins. We tried to keep the whole atmosphere light, but unspoken questions and uncertainty hung in the air.

Loosening My Grip

Sometimes God takes us into a place where everything is out in the open and there's nowhere to hide. No half-truth, no façade, no mask. And God knows that's just where we need to be so that He can do the work He wants to do. This is the place of truth. We can collapse in shame and condemnation, or we can surrender to the life-giving change. When we are willing to see ourselves as needy, we will begin to see God for who He really is. Jen Wilkins, in her book, *None Like Him*, puts it this way, "[Our limits] are reminders that keep us from falsely believing that we can be like God. When I reach the limit of my strength, I worship the One whose strength never flags."[1]

Our culture has so glorified privacy in the name of personal rights that we believe it's no one else's business that we are struggling or what we are struggling with. We believe that we need to struggle alone, in secret, because confessing our shame would only add to it.

Certainly there was no shame in the fact that we had a daughter who was in pain. My sin was found deeply rooted in a proud and independent heart that not only desired for others to see perfection in anything I touched, but which also refused to admit any need for help. In clinging to independence and perfection, I was also holding onto the shame of my evil intentions. The very thing I thought would bring shame was not shameful at all, but the hiding of it was. Only when I began to release my grip and open my hands and heart to surrender would God begin to help and heal.

My sin could only be dealt with when I was willing to bring it out into the open, exposing it to the Light. It is often in our most desperate and helpless moments that we finally let go in surrender and acknowledge our need for help—help from others in our circumstances, but more importantly, help from God in our hearts. Sometimes the thing we need most is just to recognize our need. We may have no idea what would help, we just know we need the intervening hand of God. In addition, what about letting others in on our hidden hurts? They may not be able to fix our problem or bring healing to our hearts, but they can do something even more powerful; they can pray. If I would have been humble enough early on to admit our concerns and struggles and had asked the body of Christ to call upon the One who is able, I would have not only saved myself from the mire of deep pride and shame, but also been encouraged and uplifted along the way.

> *Only when I began to release my grip and open my hands and heart to surrender would God begin to help and heal.*

Walking into this surrender would be the first step of an extended season of letting go. This was the beginning of a long list of rights God would ask me to loosen my grip on: my right to be by my husband's side in ministry, my right to walk and interact in a world familiar and comfortable to me, my freedom to involve myself in activities that brought me pleasure, and my right to a home in which I was in control. Ever the Gentle One who knows and loves, His work in my heart was preparing me for a future only He could see. Only when I learned to let go could I ever be available for the plans He had. ❧

*When we find ourselves in
circumstances and places we
think we don't belong,
God is giving us opportunity
to grow into a deeper place
of trust with Him.*

❦ 4 ❧

WE DON'T
BELONG HERE

My guard was up the day we were introduced to Pathway Family Center. I agreed to look into this place, not because I believed my daughter was an addict, but because at that moment we needed a place that could keep her safe from self-harm. We had searched the entire country looking for help. We prayed and sought counsel, and this was one of the few programs that was feasible for us in both proximity and price.

As we toured the facility, we learned just how unconventional this particular program was. The approach stepped away from just dealing with the individual and the behavior to incorporating the entire family unit. Our family, as all the others, would be required to attend counseling sessions, group meetings, and general assemblies several times a week. Although it was not technically considered an in-patient program, the "clients" were confined. They utilized a housing system referred to as "hosting" in which the families of these teens would be required to house several clients at a time, either on the weeknights or the weekend, depending on the distance you lived from the facility.

While walking around, I noticed groups of teens—girls in one area and boys in another. They were all dressed very simply—no makeup or jewelry, and no shoes (the absence of shoes was meant to discourage them from trying to run away). Many of them appeared to be at peace, even happy. I found some hope in that.

The twelve-step program Bethany would enter was based on peer involvement. It included tactics such as encouragement, verbal confrontation, shame, reward, consequences, and privilege.

A typical week for the clients looked like this: Rise early at their respective host homes, ready themselves, and arrive at the Center at 6:30 in time for group counseling. Throughout the day individual clients would meet in gender-specific groups, do school work, meet with their assigned therapists, and participate in some form of group exercise. They might also have family sessions or doctor appointments. The upper-level clients earned the right to attend a local high school; otherwise, all school-related work was done on site at the Center. At 6:00 PM, the weeknight host parents would take their group home for the night. The week culminated on Friday evenings with a general assembly of all members involved—parents, teen clients, counselors, and any family and friends who wished to attend.

Tough Love

My in-laws came with us the day we checked things out. I was so grateful to have another set of eyes and ears to observe. As it turned out, the two of them fully immersed themselves in every aspect of this program with us. Their commitment and sacrifice was a huge blessing to us and went well above the normal call of grandparents. They proved to be an encouragement not only to us and Bethany but also to the other teens in the program. We could never thank them enough for this gift.

After several hours of touring, meeting the staff, talking with some of the clients, reading the guidelines and expectations, and asking an abundance of questions, we signed on the dotted line. Most of the clients stayed anywhere from nine months to two years. We assumed Bethany would be there closer to the nine-month range.

We did not fully reveal the intensity of this program to Bethany until the night before she transferred in. Her reaction to the news was almost violent. The brunt of her anger was directed toward her daddy; the memory of it still haunts me. We made arrangements for the transfer from the hospital in the morning and then headed back home to a restless night of sleep, hoping and praying we were doing the right thing.

Drug rehab was not a place we felt we belonged, but we found ourselves there nonetheless.

Bethany was heavily medicated when we picked her up in the morning but acutely aware of what was happening. Bob's brother and his wife accompanied us as we drove Bethany to Pathway and checked her in. As it turned out, other than seeing her across the room, we would not spend any face-to-face time with her for the next six months.

Teeth Clenched, Hand Raised

We drove back down to the Center on Friday evening to witness our first group meeting. The kids sat in the front of the room facing the sea of parents and family members. It was surreal to me that my precious little girl was up there with "addicts." Every fiber of my being wanted to run up and rescue her from this place. *How did we get here? Why did we have to be here?*

The meeting began with singing, a pledge to the flag, the Lord's Prayer, and the Serenity prayer. A client, who had earned the privilege, led the group. New clients and their families were introduced and validated by a group chorus of "Love ya, Beth," "Love ya, Mom," "Love ya, Dad," "Love ya, group." Then the real fun began.

At this point, each client would stand, one at a time, and the families "confronted" and recalled the feelings associated with a past event. The client could respond and make amends, and sometimes there would be praise for the progress made, especially if the client had had a good week. The entire meeting was moderated by one of the counselors. On our first night there, we were only allowed to observe the first part of the meeting, not the confrontation part. For the next several weeks we met in a different room for new-client orientation in which we learned much about addiction, the twelve-step program, and hosting.

I was already angry when we walked in that first night. I didn't want to be there. A rehab center was not a part of my plan. So, I was kicking and screaming on the inside and now they were filling us in on the details of hosting! We were given two months to prepare, both our home and ourselves, for this monumental task.

Opened Home, Closed Heart

I am a hospitable person by nature, frequently opening my home for teas, meals, and overnight guests. But I like to do it *my way,* with extra touches of detail and kindness. God created me this way, and I find great pleasure in serving others. So even in this one area in which I felt capable and perhaps a tad special, I would be stripped bare and compelled to learn a new way to serve.

The instructions began—we would need to prepare a sleeping room for the clients. Everything had to come out, as if we had just been handed the keys to our new home: no furniture, curtains, rods, or decorations. We had to alarm any windows and put double locks on the outside of the door. Then we placed four mattresses, four fitted sheets, four blankets, and four pillows on the floor. No mints, no flowers, no snacks. Nothing. (The concept behind this was to provide a safe environment that was free from distraction and temptation.)

Next came the kitchen and bathroom. All sharps (knives, scissors, etc.), spices, aerosols, and cleaning chemicals had to be kept in a locked cabinet. The bathroom door was removed and replaced with a curtain, and the bathroom was completely emptied out other than soap, towel, and toilet paper. Every lower-level client had to be with an upper-level client or parent at all times, which meant our downstairs bathroom was the most logical place for the clients to use. However, that meant extensive renovation to add a shower. It also meant that there was always much explaining to guests who came to our house when clients weren't there as to why our bathroom had a curtain instead of a door.

Because of the intensity of the program, the early hours during the week, and the fact that our home was more than an hour and half away from the Center, we were required to host the clients over the weekends. Parents would not host their own children until they moved up to the second level of the program, which meant, in our case, I would have four strangers in my home on the weekends for the next four months. I would not be attending church, enjoying weekend outings with friends or family, or running errands. I felt that I, too, had been confined and constrained. All the unwelcome changes increased my resentment.

Accepting His Plan

The Bible records the frustrations of a group of people who found themselves in a place they didn't belong. You may be familiar with the words of Jeremiah 29:11: "'For I know the plans that I have for you,' declares the LORD, 'plans for welfare and not for evil, to give you a future and a hope.'" If we expand our reading beyond that verse, we see that these words were spoken to a group of people who were in exile, an unfamiliar and uncomfortable place of banishment. Yet God tells them to live their lives there, build relationships, construct homes, and have families there. He knew the plan and saw the bigger picture. For this reason, He assured them: "You will seek Me and find Me when you search for Me with all your heart" (Jeremiah 29:13).

When we find ourselves in circumstances and places we think we don't belong, God is giving us opportunity to grow into a deeper place of trust with Him. As we begin to walk in trust, He can work in us and through us for His glory and to further His plan. When we begin to release our own plans and walk in His, we can have true joy.

As my resentment—much of it aimed directly at Bethany—subsided, I moved toward a posture of humility. Only then was I able to see the opportunities for serving and speaking truth to this little part of the world to which I was exiled. Living in faith was much easier in the familiar environs of the church sanctuary and the Sunday school classroom than in a rehab program, but opportunity met me at every turn. We were regularly with staff, counselors, hurting families, and teenagers who, to my knowledge, did not have the hope of Jesus. Most weekends I literally had a captive audience. Outside of an occasional earned movie night, the television was rarely on, so I was able to play Christian music, read the Bible, and speak about my faith. It helped that the Bible was on the "Approved Books" list. I had the opportunity to explain passages for them and we openly discussed matters of faith. Gradually, my joy returned as I saw how God was working out "the plans He had for me." I learned many things about life, addiction, and myself. God was continuing the work He had begun in me several months earlier in our first trip to the emergency room.

Unconditional Love

Another valuable lesson I learned was that of unconditional love. My mother was an alcoholic, a fact of which I was deeply ashamed. I spent most of my adult life to that point wishing she were someone different. This built up a wall of resentment between us. I lost many years of relationship with my mother, not because of her behavior but because of my response to it. As I participated in Bethany's program and progress, able to give her unconditional love and support in spite of her behavior, the Lord helped me realize my sin in not loving my mother well. In response, I humbled myself and apologized to her. Her behavior didn't change, but our relationship did. God brought healing in the final years of my mother's life, and the regret I carried faded away.

> *When we deliberately align ourselves to His will and trust His plan, God offers peace and joy no matter our circumstances.*

We may think we can have peace and joy only when we are in comfortable surroundings with people we know. But when we deliberately align ourselves to His will and trust His plan, God offers peace and joy no matter our circumstances.

❖ ❖ ❖

Fourteen years have passed since our "exile." We still have contact with some of the families we met while Bethany was in the program at Pathway. The teens are grown now, and many are living productive and happy lives. Sadly, some of the families are grieving the same loss as our own. I am grateful for the continued opportunities to speak truth and offer hope to these friends. Pathway was a much-needed help to us in our time of crisis. As I reflect on it, I believe the most important thing this program did for us was give us time: time for me to grow spiritually and time for my heart to be prepared for new things to come.

Most of all, it gave us a little more time with Bethany. ✌

When we surrender
to God—to His love,
His compassion, His plan—
then when we need it,
He ushers in His grace.

❧ 5 ❧

GRACE TO HELP IN TIME OF NEED

As we began to contemplate life after rehab, we wondered what the future would be like for our family. *Could we ever get back to normal?* Each one of us had been changed. Bethany's choices—and our shared experiences because of them—had become part of our identity. No matter how things turned out, we had permanent scars.

Our church family had been amazing, but Bob and I began to think that we might need to step away from the pastorate for a while. Shepherding a church, while often rewarding, is highly demanding. We were drained, and we needed the time to focus on our family situation and take care of ourselves.

Time for Change

As it turned out, God had already been preparing another place for us.

About six months before we had entered the hell that was rehab, Bob and I had gone on a leadership trip with my company, Premier Designs, a direct sales jewelry business. Bob had been asked to preach at the Sunday morning worship service that closed out the week. The founder and president of the company approached Bob afterward and asked, "Could you ever see yourself in a ministry role outside of the church?" Bob answered that he was willing to do whatever God asked of him, but he couldn't see himself leaving the pastorate. One week later, Bethany broke the news to us about what had happened on the cruise. Many from Premier's home office continued to reach out to us, and once they learned what was going on with Bethany and our family, they became a regular part of our prayer, encouragement, and support team. Even though I couldn't conduct my personal business at the level I had previously, they were very understanding and helpful.

After months of prayer, counsel, and trips back and forth from Michigan to Texas, Bob accepted a staff position with Premier Designs.

In addition to leaving our precious church, the move to Texas would also separate us from Bob's family. But hardest of all, it would mean being temporarily separated from Bethany. She needed the support and stability the rehab program offered, and she needed to see it through to the end. Bob moved in the summer of 2002 while the boys and I stayed in Michigan through the fall, preparing the house to sell and continuing our involvement with Bethany in her program. Bob flew back to Michigan every other weekend.

Three days before Christmas, Bob, our sons, and I packed up our two cars and set out for Texas. On the way, we stopped to visit Bethany in the host home where she would spend Christmas. We would be traveling back and forth to visit her, and we planned for her to join us when she completed the program. We were going to prepare a new home, a new life, and a fresh start. None of this mattered, though. I felt like I had failed miserably as a mom. It tore my heart out to leave her behind in Michigan.

The January sunshine in Texas brought warmth to my heart, a gift of grace beaming down on me. I traveled to Michigan every other week to spend as much time with Bethany as possible. The boys were adjusting to new schools, and I was trying to restart my business. We were also on the hunt for a new church home. We had never had to look for a church before; as a pastor and wife, the church had always looked for us. Our search was complicated by the fact that my personal identity had been wrapped up in my role as the pastor's wife. I honestly believed it was the only thing I could do, but Christ was calling me to discover that my identity was in Him, not in a role or position. We eventually found a new church to call home. Once again, God gave us a place to belong and people who would help carry us. I was able to look back on the past year of rehab, where for weeks at a time I was away from my church family and friends, and see that God used that season in my life to graciously prepare me for this new chapter.

> *Christ was calling me to discover that my identity was in Him, not in a role or position.*

Bethany graduated from the rehab program and joined us in Texas in late March. She began the final quarter of her junior year at Flower Mound High School with her brother Scotty as her guardian and guide. She made friends who encouraged her in her newfound reality, and she became a support for many who were hurting. We were encouraged at this return to her former self. This was the Bethany I knew—my innocent, engaging, nurturing daughter. I was thrilled when I walked in on a tutoring session, as she helped a new friend understand algebra. I even overheard her giving good advice to another friend. My heart dared to hope: *she's going to get through this after all!*

Bethany got her driver's license, found a part-time job, and was doing well in school. Her fun spirit and sweet heart were returning. But in mid-May, the suicide of a casual acquaintance rattled her deeply. Then, two weeks later, one of her closer friends took her own life. Bethany had tried to help this girl, and she hadn't seen this coming. This death rocked her to her core. The downward spiral began.

Bethany began seeking out people who could help her escape the pain. She started using and cutting again, and slowly a monster emerged. Countless times I pleaded with God to give me the grace to love my girl and to see past her actions and into her hurting heart. We amped up the rules and increased her counseling sessions. All the while, fear began to wrap itself around my heart. *What if she kills herself? What will I do? What can I do?*

There were moments when it seemed as though Bethany would step out and someone else would take her place. This "other" person was unkind and hurtful, hurling words, accusations, and threats at us. Eventually, we had to expel Bethany from the house in order to protect the boys and me. I have no idea where she went when she left; I just had to be kept safe from my own daughter. Being in that situation was surreal to me. All this, and the very real possibility of another suicide attempt, kept me frozen in fear.

Daily Bread and Daily Grace

It didn't take long for the children of Israel to begin fearing for their daily sustenance even after such a miraculous deliverance from Egypt. In spite of their forgetful hearts and grumbling spirits, God graciously provided what was needed at precisely the right time. Every day. Manna. Bread. It couldn't be stored up or hoarded. Why? Because it was a daily reminder that God would show up in all His faithfulness in order to provide just what was needed for that day. It wasn't really about the gift, though. It was about the Giver. The more they obeyed Him, the more they learned to trust Him—in *all* circumstances. He gave them bread as He gives us grace, always to the degree it is needed and always at the time it is needed.

So often we fear the unknown, falsely believing we could "never endure that," whatever *that* may be. But God asks us to be ever aware of Him, not the what-ifs, remembering that He was faithful to provide yesterday and He will do so again today. Being in a place of "I could never" can actually be the beginning of humility. It's only when we realize that we truly don't have, can't do, or aren't enough, that we receive God's grace. God, the Giver, is always enough.

If the children of Israel woke up in the morning worried about what they would eat that day and just sat in their tents steeped in hunger, their hunger would not have been satisfied. God told them to get up, go outside, and gather enough manna for the day.

Like the manna that was on the ground each morning, grace is available for us. But fear and worry often keep us from experiencing (gathering) it. There is benefit and blessing from walking in faith and forgetting our fear. However, just because grace is provided doesn't mean we are instantly transported to our "promised land." The children of Israel exercised faith *while still in the wilderness.* God provided exactly what they needed, when they needed it, as they wandered. If ever we need grace, it is while we are wandering.

Empowering Grace

People often say to me, "I could never survive what you went through." And I, too, look at others' circumstances and think the same thing. When we surrender to God—to His love, His compassion, His plan—then when we need it, He ushers in His grace. I couldn't see grace, acknowledge it, or accept it when I was standing in my flood of fear. But grace was waiting to come, not when I feared the unknown, but when I really needed it, when I actually walked through the storm. As Elisabeth Elliot says, "There is no grace for your imaginations." We don't wake up one morning and decide that we will handle the cancer that is yet to be diagnosed, or the death of our spouse . . . that hasn't yet occurred. We simply aren't wired to handle what hasn't happened, and we don't have to. God doesn't give grace early or late, but always on time.

Hebrews 4:16 says, "Let us draw near with confidence to the throne of grace, so that we may receive mercy and find grace to help in time of need." It is grace alone that puts us in right standing with a holy and just God. For His child, grace is the gift of His presence that sustains, enables, empowers, comforts, and strengthens. It is grace that keeps us humble. By receiving it we are saying that we need God, that He alone is the only possible way to walk through the unthinkable. Grace allows our eyes to see the Giver of good through our tears, and His love through our loss. Grace allows us to change our perspective without invalidating our pain.

> *Grace allows our eyes to see the Giver of good through our tears, and His love through our loss.*
>
>

Are you afraid right now? Afraid for someone you know and love as you watch their choices? Afraid of the future because of the diagnosis you just received? Afraid to say yes to something God is calling you to do? Afraid of confessing a deeply buried sin? Grace can only show itself when you let go of fear and replace it with trust and obedience.

In Psalm 103, just after we are called to really ponder the "how much" of His love, forgiveness, and care in verses 11–13, we are reminded that "He Himself knows our frame; He is mindful that we are but dust." (14). It is the humble who also recognizes her frame, and in so doing, invites grace in. It is in the surrender of "I can't!" when God steps in and graciously says, "But I can."

In his book *New Morning Mercies*, Paul David Tripp writes,

> *For the believer, fear is always God-forgetful.... Next time you face the unexpected, a moment of difficulty you really don't want to go through, remember that such a moment doesn't picture a God who has forgotten you, but one who is near to you and doing in you a very good thing. He is rescuing you from thinking that you can live the life you were meant to live while relying on*

the inadequate resources of your wisdom, experience, righteousness, and strength; and he is transforming you into a person who lives a life shaped by radical God-centered faith. (January 8 and 9)

June and July proved to be a tumultuous time for us, yet we relied on God's grace. Each day provided us opportunity to exercise faith in Him, and each day He was faithful. As we focused on God, He continued to increase our trust, which in turn led to peace. From grace to faith, trust to peace, we walked a hard road with Him always at our side. ✍

*God gave me
a gift that day.
He removed my fear.*

~ 6 ~

PEACE THAT PASSES UNDERSTANDING

A shroud of terror hangs on parents whose child struggles with suicidal thoughts and tendencies. Our minds constantly rehearse the what-ifs. We analyze every conversation for clues of destructive actions. We try to stay one step ahead. Gone are any carefree interactions with our child, of being together just for the pleasure of one another's company. We are always on guard.

A Hopeful Respite

In late July 2003, Bob and I attended the national conference for Premier Designs. We were apprehensive about both of us being gone from home at the same time, but our responsibilities required it. To be honest, I was looking forward to a respite from the storm that had become life with Bethany. Fortunately, the conference was just an hour's drive away. Since we had to stay at the convention center overnight—Bob's team was responsible for much of the weekend's activities—we made appropriate arrangements for Bethany and our boys. I prepared the house as thoroughly as I could by securing all medications and sharp objects, and then

57

made sure that Bethany would be watched over by her accountability group.

I was thrilled to have my mind on something other than
keeping my daughter safe from herself. I had enjoyed a full day
of respite, and we were nearing the end of the conference. I was
abruptly pulled back to reality, however, when I received a text
to call home right away. I slipped out into the hallway and made
the call; Bethany had been taken to the hospital by ambulance.
*How in the world am I going to find Bob? This is the Fort Worth
Convention Center, and he could be anywhere!*
But God is always one step ahead of us. Just
as I hung up the phone, from down a long
corridor came one of the men on Bob's team.
I explained what was happening and he was
able to help me find Bob right away.

> *We needed to
> be armed with
> strength that
> comes only
> through prayer.*

We headed off to yet another emergency
room. Instead of making phone calls on our
drive, we prayed. We knew we would need
more than details of the circumstances when
we entered Bethany's room; we needed to be armed with strength
that comes only through prayer.

When we arrived at the hospital, we were directed to a large
private room. There our daughter lay, once again, in sterile surroundings that seemed to swallow up her warm spirit. She was
alone, mostly unconscious, with tubes and wires attached all over.
We made our way to the bedside, waiting for her to wake up just
a little. We wanted her to know that we were both there for her.
Once we exchanged a few comforting glances and words, Bob left
to attend to paperwork and to see to the boys who had arrived at
the hospital by this time.

I stood by Bethany's bed grasping for words to say to this precious girl who was becoming such a stranger to me. "I shouldn't
have gone," I said. It was all I could come up with. She whispered,

"Mom, you don't think I wouldn't have done this if you had been home?" Then she rolled over and drifted back to sleep.

The room was large, as emergency rooms go, and her bed was off to one side. The lights were turned off, almost as if they had given up on her—another troubled teenager. Insert the tubes and IVs, hook up the monitors, and then leave her alone. *Don't they know she's someone's little girl? Don't they know she's my little girl? She's hurting! She thinks this is the only way to stop the pain.* I couldn't understand her actions or how she felt, but to shove her into a dimly lit corner surely wouldn't help.

A Heart Prepared

On the other side of the room was a small counter and chair. I had my back to Bethany's bed—there was a gap between us of about eight feet—and my chair was illuminated by a single dim light. My mind was going a thousand different directions when my thoughts were interrupted by, of all things … peace. It was as if the Holy Spirit had entered my mind and ministered to me with words of truth. This was a pivotal moment, and I felt compelled to write down what He was speaking to my heart. I pulled a small legal pad from my purse and began to write—

> *It was as if the Holy Spirit had entered my mind and ministered to me with words of truth.*

What I Know

1. God makes no mistakes.

2. God will never leave me or forsake me.

3. God will never lead me where His grace cannot keep me—my grace is sufficient for you—most gladly will I rejoice in my infirmities that when I am weak then He is strong.

4. Count it all joy when you fall into various testing, knowing this: the trial of your faith will bring patience, and patience, when it is complete, will bring forth a crown of glory—one that I can cast at His feet in glory.

5. It is not His will that any should perish, but that all should come to repentance.

6. My God shall supply all my needs according to His riches in Christ Jesus.

7. The peace that passes all understanding shall keep my heart and mind.

8. All things work together for good to them who are called and to them who love God.

9. God knows the plans He has for my life—plans to give me a future and to prosper me, not to harm me.

10. God has created Bethany in His image and she has worth and value because she has been fearfully and wonderfully made.

11. Whosoever calls upon the name of the Lord shall be saved.

12. Forgiveness is a gift from God, and that God extends His forgiveness to Bethany—she needs to accept that and "confess" (agree) and be cleansed. Though our sins be as scarlet they can be white as snow.

13. Jesus came to give us life (eternal—spiritual) and to give it to us abundantly (physical—emotional).

14. I don't have to give thought about tomorrow—God has planned my future before the foundation of the world.

15. My heavenly Father loves my daughter so much that He gave His precious Son to die for her and to offer her the priceless gift of peace, joy, and eternal life.

16. I have no regrets of following my faithful God, and I know He is in control!

17. I love Bethany and I wish I could help her.

Truth. God's Word had been tucked away in my heart over the years. His Spirit used these truths to administer healing and peace to my heart in that moment when I needed it most. God Almighty who knows me personally, understood my pain, and cared enough to show up and offer me help. How I praise Him!

I have kept the four pages of that pad all these years as a reminder that my God is real. He is true. He can be trusted. To many it may seem unlikely that a bunch of garbled Bible verses could bring such comfort, but I believe the Bible and am comforted by it because I have seen it come alive in my heart as well as in the hearts and lives of people I love. Each time I experience His truth or see it transform lives, my faith in Him deepens.

I am aware that this next statement may sound strange and perhaps even shocking; however, there was another "message" I received from God that day: "Bethany will be successful in her attempts, it will be soon, and I will be with you."

It was not an audible message, and neither was it disheartening. I didn't walk away resigned to doom and dread. I just felt like God was preparing me. We continued to fight for Bethany. I still made phone calls to different counseling agencies and therapy clinics. We still took every precaution in our home and kept her near. We continued to pray for her, for healing, for Satan to release control of her mind. We still did all that, but God gave me a gift that day. He removed my fear.

That Day

It was a Wednesday, just three days after bringing Bethany home from the hospital. The conference was over and family and friends were going back to their homes. All the activity that had been a distraction was coming to an end. We would have to face our reality; we would have to face her, confront her, plead with her. *Why is this your only way out?*

I took my sister and niece to the airport in the morning and then returned home. I put my kid gloves back on, walked up the stairs, turned the corner, paused, took a deep breath, put my hand on the doorknob, prayed, and entered.

"Good morning, Sunshine!" I said with a smile on my face and a lilt in my voice. I walked around her bed to the side where there was very little room. I bent down to give her a hug and clumsily pulled the long purple sash off the curtain rod and onto the floor. *Why did I go to that side of the bed?*

"What are you trying to do, Mom, destroy my room?" she asked. She's wasn't mad, she was actually joking with me. I glanced up at the sash precariously hanging from the rod, and I thought, *She's going to hang herself with that.* The thought darted in my mind then back out again.

"Sorry about that, Bethany. Let me fix it."

"It's okay, Mom."

And I left.

✦ ✦ ✦

Bethany's senior year of high school would be starting in less than a month and we had much to discuss. The recent escalation in her suicide attempts told us she was going backward in her healing and would require an alternative approach to the school year. We had made some inquiries through personal visits and phone calls, and we had an important counseling appointment set up for the next day, one that had been months in the making. We were eager for this appointment with a group of Christian doctors. Surely they could help us.

The boys were out with their friends, so it was just Bethany and me at home. Our activity was mundane, almost normal. I actually felt a sense of ease in our casual conversation throughout the morning. As I applied my makeup, she sat cross-legged on the floor in my bathroom just talking. It had been so long since we had had that kind of togetherness that my heart danced with the simple delight of it. I desperately wanted to believe that things were getting better, but deep down I felt that this was the calm before the storm.

I needed to confront her about a set of car keys that she had secretly duplicated and was keeping hidden from us. After the weekend stay at the hospital, we had removed all her privileges, including her car. But she had prepared for such a time as this; those keys and that car would be her escape.

Bethany wanted to visit one of her friends, so after assuring me that her friend's mother would be home, I reluctantly agreed to take her there for a short visit. Before we left, I broached the subject of her future. "After dinner tonight, you, Dad, and I need to talk about your future."

"I don't have a future," she said.

God, help me, help me say the right words, I quickly prayed. Surely I could convince her of her worth, her value, how much we loved her, how much God loved her. I tried to reassure Bethany that we would get through this.

She looked at me through sad eyes that somehow still sparkled, and then I momentarily walked away to get something from another room. I was gone for no more than thirty seconds, but when I returned, Bethany was gone and "another" was there. (For weeks I had been feeling as though "another" was coming and going in and out of Bethany's person.) She was still standing in the same place, but Bethany was gone. The sparkle was gone. The eyes, her beautiful eyes, were dead.

"You don't love me! You don't even like me!" she screamed.

Where did she go? This didn't even sound like her voice. She wasn't sad, she was angry. I couldn't grasp what my eyes were seeing or my mind was experiencing at that moment. I was confused to see the same body standing in front of me but the person inside was so completely different. It was as if God had hold of her heart but Satan had hold of her mind.

I replied, "Of course I love you! We all love you!" But my heart was pleading inside, *Please, please, please come back! Please believe me! Why can't you believe me? Where are you? Why do you leave so suddenly? Where do you go and who is this left standing in your place?* I had so many questions, but I knew she couldn't answer them. *God! Why can't we fix her? Why are we not enough for her?* I had questions for Him as well.

Tomorrow. Those doctors... They will begin to fix her. Hold on for tomorrow.

✦ ✦ ✦

I drove Bethany to her friend's house, confirming the mom would be home the whole time. *It will be okay,* I thought. *Perhaps some time with them will help her cool down.* She got out of the car and I said, "Remember to be home for dinner. And Bethany, I love you."

"I love you, too, Mom." And she shut the door.

I went home and cleaned. Cleaned the house. Cleaned the house thoroughly, because that's what I do. Stress, stress, stress... Must be perfect. Clean, clean, clean. I cooked dinner, set the table, we gathered. No Bethany. We prayed. Still no Bethany. We began to eat. The door opened and Bethany stormed in. She threw the set of duplicate keys on the table and stomped out of the room and up the stairs.

And there she died. She ushered herself into eternity with a purple sash.

The Presence of Peace

This act. So final. No turning back, no time to try a different approach. Her struggle over, ours to escalate as we navigate life through the wreckage and the aftermath. For my own sanity, peace had to become more than just an ethereal idea—it had to be palpable. For a while, the shock and numbness carried me along; but after it wore off, I could look back and see the presence of the God of peace had been my constant companion and would continue to walk beside me through this valley.

In her book *One Thousand Gifts*, Ann Voskamp writes,

> *Trust is the bridge from yesterday to tomorrow, built with planks of thanks. Remembering frames up gratitude. Gratitude lays out the planks of trust. I can walk the planks—from known to unknown—and know: He holds.... Without trust in the good news of Jesus, without trust in the good news of God's saving work even in this moment, without an active, moment-by-moment trust in the good news of an all-sovereign, all-good God, how can we claim to fully believe? This is the trust I lack: to know that if disaster strikes, He carries me even there.*[1]

I have a sign in my office that reads, "In Acceptance there is Peace." Learning and choosing to accept even my daughter's suicide has given me peace—the kind that surpasses my own understanding and even my need for the why to be answered.

I also believe that Bethany is at peace. Her death is not what gives her peace, but rather her decision many years ago to trust God's grace on her behalf—His Way, Jesus Christ. Christ is her peace and He can be yours as well.

✦ ✦ ✦

My prayer is that you would invite Him to lead you as you walk through your own journey of pain and ultimate healing. As you recount His faithfulness to you, and the promises of His Word, you will begin to experience peace that only comes from resting and trusting in Him. He not only promises peace to those who trust Him, He assures us of His presence as we trust. To quote C. J. Mahaney, may each of us be "transformed from questioning to praying, from confusion to certainty, from being perplexed to fully trusting in God."[2] ℘

> *He not only promises peace to those who trust Him, He assures us of His presence as we trust.*

In the seemingly insignificant to the very profound moments, I always want to see God's hand at work.

ᴄ7ᴅ

CHERISH THE MOMENT

My husband has an unusual talent. He can take any familiar tune and improvise new lyrics on the spot. I haven't always accepted his talent as a gift. In fact, in some cases I thought it was a subtle form of blasphemy.

Bob was raised in church, so most of the tunes he's familiar with are old hymns; to me, the words of those hymns are almost sacred. My husband's verses are more like reflections or observations of life happening around him at any given moment. So, what you get is a spontaneous commentary of life in song, much like a musical or an opera, but more along the lines of Monty Python than Andrew Lloyd Webber.

One day I found myself humming a tune, and then ... I started singing words that I knew weren't the right words. This bothered me on several levels. First, I was slipping into my husband's "talent"; second, I couldn't remember the real words; and third, I couldn't even recall where I had heard the melody. Finally, it came to me—it was our song, Bethany's and mine.

I love music. I always have. I was raised on it. It was a huge part of my childhood and home. I majored in music in college and continue to be blessed by this beautiful gift from God. So naturally, I made sure my children were introduced to uplifting and wholesome music. One of our family favorites was a children's musical series called Patch the Pirate. Each episode presented an adventure of Patch and his crew, featuring biblical themes and delivering lessons in Christian living. From one of those episodes came the song, "Cherish the Moment"; I loved it so much that I wanted Bethany to learn it so we could sing it together some day. That day came on Mother's Day, 1991.

Tugging At Our Heartstrings

The song was perfect for Mother's Day because it was a reflective duet, tugging on the heart strings to cherish the fleeting moments of childhood and parenthood. So, on that day, with bouncy blond curls and dressed in little lavender frills, Bethany made her singing debut. Mom and Dad were so proud! The church folks beamed while wiping away tears, and Grandpa caught it all on video.

We never reprised our duet. Perhaps five was her peak, or more likely, in her pre-adolescent days, the thought of a public performance with Mom was just too embarrassing. Nevertheless, in my heart that would forever be "our song," and I, indeed, cherished that moment.

The years came and went as they do. The struggles of teenage life overshadowed those precious childhood times, and my mind had long since pushed that moment into the memory archives. Until one day, just weeks before Bethany left us.

She was lucid and chipper that morning—very Bethany—as she approached me with a big grin and twinkling eyes. She had just returned from a visit to Michigan, a visit that had ended prematurely and badly. So, her demeanor was a surprising change from just a few hours before when we had picked her up at the airport. We were indeed learning to cherish the moments of brightness and lightness, because they came unexpectedly and then vanished just as quickly. They were the moments that kept our hope alive.

Bethany took my hand and led me into her brother Ricky's room, where I found him grinning too. She instructed me to lie down on the bed and close my eyes. I obeyed. Then she sat down next to me and took my hand in hers. "Mom, just listen. I have a surprise for you." Click.

From the first gentle notes of the piano introduction, the tears began to roll down my face. Then her sweet tender five-year-old voice began to sing...

> *Read my book, rub my back, Mommy, listen to my prayer*
> *Let me sit in your lap, Daddy, fly me through the air*
> *Throw a ball, make a snack, can we go to the park?*
> *Tuck me in, hold me close, I'm afraid of the dark.*
>
> *Cherish the moment, soon you'll be apart*
> *Cling to the memory, clasp it to your heart*
> *Soon comes the day when you'll have no child to hold*
> *So, cherish, cherish the moment.**

I remained on the bed for the entirety of the song, tears streaming down my cheeks the whole time, and then collapsed into sobs when it was over. Bethany hugged me tight with one of her bear hugs and proceeded to explain how and where she had acquired this treasured gift—from Grandpa who had kept a copy of the recording from that Mother's Day so many years before. In that moment, that memory, that hug, a tiny bit of sanity pushed into our living hell. Refreshing drops of rain on the tired and parched soul of mine.

Arrangements

The days after Bethany's death were blurry and numbing, yet we had a funeral to prepare. Write an obituary... plan the service... order flowers for the casket... answer the phone... answer the door... get out of bed... try to keep it together...

---

* *Cherish the Moment* by Ron Hamilton. Copyright © 1990 by Majesty Music, Inc. All rights reserved; used by permission.

God sent several of His ministers to us in the form of precious friends who lovingly surrounded our family. They took care of so many details. Two of those special friends approached me with the idea of a video picture montage of Bethany's life. I said that I trusted them to handle it and directed them to a trunk of unorganized photos.

Soon one of these friends came back and asked, "What about a song? What was one of her favorite songs?" I had no idea how to answer; I couldn't think. Later she came back downstairs and handed me a cassette tape, saying, "I found this under the couch while I was vacuuming. What is it?" I looked at the treasure in her hands and said, "It's the song for the picture montage."

Three weeks earlier that cassette tape had vanished, but now, at just the right time, it had come back to me. The paramedics had moved the couch while attending to Bethany the day before. Apparently, the tape had been there under the couch the whole time. Seeing the label, "Cherish the Moment," was both a slap in the face *and* a gentle reminder that God is good. He is concerned about the details of His children's lives. He is real, He is acquainted with our pain, and He cares. He gives us good and sweet things to enjoy. He gives us pleasant memories. Not only was the discovery of that lost tape—and the treasured song it contained—a source of great joy to me in this very dark moment, it would also prove to be a great comfort to all those who mourned with us at her funeral in Michigan.

✦ ✦ ✦

Since we had lived in Texas such a short time, we decided to bury Bethany in Michigan. However, we chose to have two funerals, the first one in Texas, to give our friends there the opportunity to grieve. Most people there had only known Bethany a very short time or had only been introduced to her briefly. They weren't grieving a personal loss so much as they were grieving for us. Because of that, they cared for things objectively and efficiently, yet also very lovingly. We had three speakers at the Texas funeral, two of them had met her only a few times. They spoke to our needs and offered words of encouragement to those who would support us.

The third, Glenn Stewart, "Pastor Studu," as Bethany had affectionately called him, was a longtime friend. He used the most beautiful analogy when he spoke—Cinderella. With her golden locks, the picture fit Bethany so well. Cinderella was beautiful and had the love of her parents. She wanted for nothing. But one day, tragedy struck, and she found herself under the control of a good-for-nothing substitute of care, the evil stepmother. But, in His love, the Prince took her away to live with Him, happily ever after.

This analogy still gives me comfort.

The Comfort of Memories

God gives us moments. Some are painful, some sweet. It's up to us to steward the moments well, to cherish them, and also to grow from them. These moments give us ample opportunity to learn more about just how much God cares for and loves us. They help us see the beauty in the good and the bad. As we tuck away these precious seeds into the soil of our heart, they can return as lush flowers filling a garden of praise to a faithful God whose care never wavers.

In his book *A Grace Disguised*, Jerry Sittser says that deep sorrow "can make us more alive to the present moment." Grief can actually enrich our lives—if we let it. Sittser goes on to say:

> *God gives us moments. Some are painful, some sweet.*

> *This view of the present makes us aware of the wonder of life itself, gives us a keen awareness of the world around us, and deepens our appreciation for each moment as it comes to us. Even in loss and grief, we can choose to*

embrace the miracle of each moment and receive the
gifts of grace that come to us all the time. This present
moment, this eternal now, is sacred because, however
painful, it is the only time we have to be alive and to
know God. The past is gone, the future not yet here.
But the present is alive to us.[1]

I pray that I will be faithful in seeing and hearing God in the present moments, whether they are pleasant or painful. I will look for His hand, for His gifts of love and beauty, for the joy in relationships that reflect a personal God, for the delight that rises in my soul when I am joyful, and for the comfort He provides when I face heartache. In the seemingly insignificant to the very profound moments, I always want to see God's hand at work.

One grieving father said this upon learning that all ten of his children had been killed: "The LORD gave and the LORD has taken away. Blessed be the name of the LORD" (Job 1:21). His is a remarkable story of responding to loss, of running to God and not away from Him, even though he had so many questions and complaints.

+ + +

Like Job, we can acknowledge the truth we know about our God and still completely shut down in the midst of our grief. This is a natural reaction to trauma. When I was overwhelmed in my pain, I found comfort in remembering two things:

1. God never promised me life free from pain. Because of sin, just like everyone else's, my story—on this side of eternity—is riddled with heartache and misfortune.

2. Because of sin, even the precious moments, God's good gifts, are temporary and fleeting, except for one: the gift of salvation. Our reconciliation to God through the work of Jesus is the only gift we are offered that will last forever.

Even in my loss, I can join Job in saying, "Blessed be the name of the Lord." I do not deny myself the luxury of grief, but I stand firm in my perspective of the gifts God gives—both temporal and eternal. Because of this, I have adopted an "in the moment" attitude of living. The moments I share here with my loved ones are indeed precious to me, so I do my best to be very present and soak them in, for I am not promised another moment like it.

Furthermore, learning to widen my range of sight from the here and now to eternity enables me to endure in my suffering and pain.

We can, in our losses here on earth, learn to appreciate the good and cling to the better that is to come. Even in our pain, God gives us pleasant memories and present awareness of His gentle loving-kindness, whether it's in the form of a breathtaking sunset or a need that is met unexpectedly. Whatever it may be, it cannot surpass the greatest and most important gift of restoring us to eternal fellowship with Him. We can and should see that as a true blessing. Let's learn to look for the moments, those times when God reaches out and says, "I love you." Cherish the moment, clasp it to your heart, and remember that God is good. He is always good.

> *Learning to widen my range of sight from the here and now to eternity enables me to endure in my suffering and pain.*
>
>

*Every experience we
face has the potential to
make us an extension
of God's grace.*

❧ 8 ❧

A Teacup Full
of Memories

All of the "firsts" we must face after losing a loved one are
challenging: the first holiday season, the first birthday (ours
and theirs), the first wedding anniversary, and—most dreadful of
all—the first "death anniversary." These days bring a barrage of
memories, some painful and some pleasant.

The cold reality of firsts hit me while cooking Thanksgiving
dinner without Bethany. Just the year before she had run down
the stairs, proclaiming, "I won't eat all day till the big dinner is on
the table!" Thanksgiving was her favorite. Still, I wanted to hold
to tradition as best I could, so I began unpacking the Christmas
decorations later in the day... and came across her stocking. That
was an emotional day, to say the least.

Anticipating the first Christmas season after her death, my
in-laws suggested the family should celebrate in a neutral place.
So, we spent two weeks with most of Bob's family in Orlando,
Florida. Not having to go back to so many family memories in
Michigan, facing that setting without her, was a blessing. For
two weeks the brothers and sisters and cousins and grandparents
enjoyed a reprieve, the sunshine, Disney World, and each other. It
really was a lovely time.

Turn Back Time

Several of the adults decided to ring in the New Year at the Magic Kingdom under the glorious displays of fireworks. We watched the Main Street parade, then the countdown to 2004 began: 10...9...8...I started to panic. I felt myself starting to hyperventilate. Stinging tears flooded my eyes and deep sobs overtook me ... *Wait! Stop! No! We can't leave 2003!*

I was completely caught off-guard by this attack of emotions that flooded over me in the middle of a celebration. But I just couldn't bear the thought that 2004 would never have her in it. I wanted to hang onto 2003. A new year was a slap of reality—the world was moving along without her.

The more years that go by, the further away we are from Bethany, or so it seems. And I sometimes worry, *What if she's forgotten?* "Those who suffer loss live suspended between a past for which they long and a future for which they hope."[1]

After Bethany died, I was frustrated that I could only recall the tumultuous events of the recent past. I could not bring to my memory anything pleasant about her, which heaped piles of guilt upon my grief. My memories would serve me better later, but for the time being they were troubling.

Some people try to shut out their memories, as if doing so would help them to hurt less, or perhaps even change reality. I know of families that remove all signs of the deceased person, refusing to even mention their name. Frankly, I cannot understand that response. It seems to invalidate a life, never pausing to be grateful for the role that person played. But the opposite response sometimes surfaces as well: refusing to change anything and keeping the loved one's personal items just as they were, as if the person might come back and need them again. It seems that a balance can and must be found between those two responses.

There are wonderful and tender ways to remember our loved ones. Keeping mementos of their belongings may make us feel close to them. Celebrating their life on special days, honoring their memory through donations to special causes, and speaking of them are some of the ways to keep their life close to heart. We have chosen a subtle approach: every room in our home displays a touch of Bethany. Only a few people recognize these or know their meaning, but it's a simple way that I have chosen to keep her memory alive and close to my heart.

A Coat and a Collection

Bethany had her daddy's build; at sixteen she was already taller and bigger than me. Even so, I've kept some of her clothing, and when the weather turns cool in the fall, I often wear her jacket. To me, being enveloped in her coat is as close as I can come to getting another hug from her. It's a simple thing, but it brings her close.

There is also a special way that I honor Bethany's memory each year on her birthday. It started quite by accident.

As a little girl, Bethany loved to dress up at Grandma's house and have tea parties with her cousins. My mother-in-law had a beautiful collection of teacups, so she often accommodated her granddaughters' desires by allowing the use of her teacups for these special occasions.

Bethany's seventeenth birthday came six weeks after her death. I went out that day to keep myself busy and to buy something for her birthday that would commemorate her life. I really had no idea what exactly I was looking for, but as I wandered through a Christian bookstore, I suddenly saw the perfect gift—a teacup.

The teacup represented Bethany well and on many levels. She could be a princess one day and a jester the next—the patterns on the cup mirrored her multi-faceted personality—and she had a warm, hospitable spirit. (A neighbor once called to tell me what a sweet and thoughtful daughter I have. It seems that Bethany had baked cookies, written a note, and delivered both to this neighbor—all without me knowing. She was ten years old at the time.)

The teacup also represented the delicacy that had character-ized Bethany after her life-altering experience on the cruise. She had indeed become very fragile, requiring that she be handled with care.

I have carefully selected a teacup in her honor every birthday since. In fact, Bob and I often take a weekend getaway to search for just the right cup. It's a way for us to be together in our grief while honoring the memory of our daughter.

Over the years friends and family members have contributed to my teacup collection. My mother-in-law has even sent me some of Bethany's favorites from their tea party days. In one sense it makes me sad to have such a sizable collection, but when that sadness seized me one year, instead of allowing myself to dwell on the gloomy side of it, I decided to plan something positive.

When life gives you teacups, have a tea party! And that's what I did. I invited my friends over for a celebration of her life. Most of my new friends never knew Bethany, but they celebrated her just the same. There was no program or agenda, I just focused on the sweet fellowship and rejoiced to see how my life had been blessed by the people God had brought into it. I talked about Bethany, got the photo albums out, and shared some fun memories and even stories about how or where some of the teacups were acquired. Some of my friends who lived too far away to join us decided to have a cup of tea in her memory. Some still do this each year on her birthday.

Over the years, as my pain has lessened, I have used this day to invite a handful of friends over who have lost loved ones within that year. It's a way to reflect on the fact that God has strengthened me over the years and is a sweet way to show love and comfort to those whose grief is fresh.

These tea parties have helped me realize that it is possible to live a life of gratitude on the other side of loss. It's not only possible, it is essential. God can use our brokenness and pain. Our hearts can be strengthened when we take the time to celebrate all the beautiful people He has given us the opportunity to know and love. Can we still be allowed to mourn? Of course! But if we stay in our pain or somehow wish that life were not the way it is, we miss the chance to grow, to continue to live, to deepen our dependence on and relationship with our loving God.

When the Numbness Wears Off

What happens though, when like the Tin Man, you feel as though you have no heart? Sometimes, especially after loss, you may wander around feeling as though you have no heart at all. You may feel quite empty inside, void of any emotion toward anything or anyone, save your own loss. It may be months before you can respond to Scripture, sing worship songs, or enjoy fellowship. This is normal … for a while. I experienced all these things, just going through motions, trying to survive. But this is certainly not a healthy place to park.

When we stay in the "no heart" zone we are essentially shielding ourselves from further pain, from ever connecting again, trying to avoid increased hurt. We turn our heart away from God, the Comforter, we take away His opportunity to heal and ultimately be glorified. Instead, we focus on how we are going to protect ourselves. Can we even imagine what blessings we forfeit when we respond this way? Friendships, community with the Body of Christ, opportunity to be a testimony to God's healing work, and even the joy of living. (Yes, there will be joy again.)

James 1:2-4 reminds us to "Consider it pure joy, my brothers and sisters, whenever you face trials of many kinds, because you know that the testing of your faith produces perseverance. Let perseverance finish its work so that you may be mature and complete, not lacking anything" (NIV). When we are finally able to be thankful, not necessarily *for* the loss, but for the work God is doing in us *through* the pain of the loss, we are on our way to this kind of "pure joy." The admonition here is not to embrace the pain, but rather to embrace the results of going through pain. Every experience we face has the potential to make us an extension of God's grace. My heart's desire is that I would learn to suffer well, so that I can shine a light on the glory and power of my Lord.

✦ ✦ ✦

There were other things I did after Bethany left us that helped me through my grief, things that were not easy. I didn't do these perfectly, but they helped me move forward.

1. I continued my daily quiet time with God, even though for a while I couldn't absorb much of what I read. Still I knew this discipline would keep me connected to my Comforter as well as continue to store up truth in my heart, which I would need in order to face the ongoing rampages of grief. I needed truth in front of my mind when I was bombarded by doubt, fear, or despair.

2. I learned to stay open to the help and company of my friends even when I wanted to be alone. When we suffer loss or tragedy, many of our friends have little idea what to say or do. They grope with awkward words to try to soothe, knowing that nothing they say will change our circumstances. We grievers must extend grace to them and be thankful for those who just simply show up. That is how my friends demonstrated that they cared, and I needed to love them back by inviting them into my pain. Isolation was the alternative, and that was dangerous.

3. One of the more practical disciplines I took on was to do something measurable every day—measurable, not remarkable. This helped me feel normal. Every day I did at least one thing for myself, one thing for someone else, and one thing productive. These were not monumental tasks, perhaps a bubble bath, an encouraging email to a friend, and a load of laundry. But it kept me putting one foot in front of the other. It kept me sane.

4. I determined to talk about Bethany. I couldn't stand the thought of her memory being tucked away in a corner. I also knew from the experiences of others that this would make

people more at ease if I brought up the subject. I found that my willingness to bring her into conversation helped people relax. I had to make sure she wasn't the only thing I talked about, of course. However, talking about her helped remind me of who she was, who she had been. She was a wonderful part of my life, a treasure from God.

5. I prayed for a humble and compassionate heart. The world didn't stop hurting the day my daughter died. I asked for eyes to see others' pain and the strength to serve them. I had many days when I just didn't feel like walking alongside someone else in the valley. I would get angry when someone would tell me they knew what I was going through because their cat just died. (True story.) How can we show compassion when we so easily want to compare? When we hurt, we just want to be validated, don't we? We want others to recognize that our pain is legitimate. I think this is what it means to "weep with those who weep." As God comforts us, He gives us not only the strength but also the opportunity to extend that comfort to others.

6. One last thing I did was to begin journaling my heartaches, my fears, my tears, and the things God was teaching me. This was new to me, and it was so helpful. Getting my thoughts out of my head and onto the page helped me look at things more objectively. Also, it proved to be such an encouragement down the road when I would read through and find that God truly had been beside me through the darkest shadows of the valley.

❖ ❖ ❖

Grieving is not fun, it is not easy, but it can draw us closer to the heart of God. Grief transports us to a new world, a new normal where we find our joy again, whether in the daily grind or the celebrations of life—in an old coat or a new teacup. May we find God, our Comforter, in the midst of that new world, and may we rejoice over all the beauty of the loved ones we've lost, as well as those we still have. ℘

*Slowly I emerge from
the darkness of my own
prison of grief into the
light of His love.*

ᘒ 9 ᘒ

FORGIVENESS

Do I really need to forgive someone I'll never meet? That question surfaced in my heart and mind repeatedly, and it burned.

Since the day Bethany had told us about being assaulted, we had basically lived in survival mode, trying to keep her alive and hold our family together. I had given little thought to the man who had done this to her. I had stuffed those thoughts and emotions so deep that they didn't resurface until years after her death.

As I became aware of what was happening to me, I began to view my life as a long-neglected lawn. What had at one time been green, lush, shady, and welcoming (not that I had ever been perfect) was now overrun with weeds and dotted with bare spots. Unforgiveness and bitterness had done that to me. I was angry, fearful, and resentful. Ironically, I felt entitled to hang on to those feelings. The roots of my pain ran deep. Much deeper than I had realized.

✦ ✦ ✦

In his book, *The Gift of Forgiveness*, Charles Stanley defines forgiveness as "the act of setting someone free from an obligation to you that is a result of a wrong done against you." He goes on to say that forgiveness involves three elements: "injury, a debt resulting from the injury, and a cancellation of the debt."[1] Oftentimes we refuse to cancel the debt because the wrong done to us hurt too badly, the effect of the wrongdoing was too great, or we don't see any change in the one who wronged us that would make them worthy of our forgiveness.

My feelings of anger, bitterness, and unforgiveness began to surface as I participated in an organized Bible study. I knew God was leading me to a place I didn't want to go—forgiving the man who took my Bethany from me. So I wrestled with God, arguing the technicalities as I saw them, rationalizing my anger with "facts" such as, "If they don't ask for it, I'm under no obligation to forgive." But, in my spirit, I knew that my unforgiving heart kept no one in bondage but myself.

✦ ✦ ✦

At the same time I was wrestling with all of this, I was also preparing for a mission trip to Africa. (God's timing is spot-on.) Bob and I would be visiting several ministries in two different countries to assess their needs and offer encouragement to their staff. One of those ministries was International Needs in Ghana (INGH), West Africa. We were already familiar with what they did and were eager to see it firsthand. Many years before, a representative of this ministry had visited our church in Michigan, and the things we learned about that work had left a deep impression on Bethany.

God would do a deep work in my heart on this trip, so let me provide some context for how that came about, or, I should say, how God brought it about. For that, you'll need to know a little about the work that INGH does. Here's a description, written by one of their staff members.

> The work of International Needs in Ghana targets the horrific practice of "Trokosi," which is the involuntary servitude of young virgin girls being given to a fetish priest. This priest is highly revered because he serves as a mediator between the spirit and the living and worships and seeks favor from the god in the shrine.

When someone feels wronged they go to this fetish priest and he decides whether the "crime" requires atonement. If he determines that it does, the family of the accused wrongdoer must give their virgin daughter to the fetish priest. They turn their daughter over to the local shrine, believing that if they do not, the gods will wreak vengeance on their family or entire community. Many times the girl does not even know what the offense was that brought her to the shrine.

There is a ceremony when a girl is brought to the shrine. She is ceremoniously walked to the shrine and stripped of her clothes and her beads, and her shoes are removed. She is then given a loincloth of a certain color that distinguishes her so people will avoid social interaction with her. Her soul now belongs to the gods. She is condemned to a lifelong servitude of hard labor, rape, and perpetual childbearing.

Punishment is harsh in the shrine. The girl is beaten to the satisfaction of the fetish priest for reasons such as not completing her work properly, not completing chores, refusing to have sex with the priest, or refusing anything he commands. Other punishments include confinement and starvation.

As a result of being raped by the fetish priest, the girl bears his children, perhaps four or more. When she gives birth, the girl is not given any assistance or medical attention; she is only helped by other Trokosi. She is then sent back to work almost immediately, with her baby tied to her back. Her life is dehumanizing; she may live this way for her whole life.

In 1991, under the leadership of Reverend Walter Pimpong, INGH became the catalyst for liberating the girls, women, and children being held in bondage by the fetish priests. Through years of negotiation, INGH has set thousands of women and children free, securing agreements from the fetish priests that the shrine will not take any new slaves.

When the women and children are freed, they have no education and no personal identity. Many families do not want them back because of their fear of the gods.

In 1995, INGH established a vocational center in Adidome, in the Volta region of Ghana, where women receive rehabilitation after liberation so they can take care of themselves and their children. They receive emotional counseling, Bible teaching, and learn a trade such as baking, catering, hairdressing, soap making, and dressmaking. They learn how to read and write, run a business, and are provided a start-up kit and microloans to start their business.

The children are enrolled in a village school where the staff members care for them. Because of the ministry to the Trokosi, entire villages have been liberated from bondage to the fetish priests and their gods and are now worshipping the true and living God.*

During our time at INGH, we were able to witness the induction of a new group of women recently released from bondage. Through the work of this ministry, local churches and Bible schools are built in the villages, and the hope of Jesus Christ is taught and lived out. What we experienced during the welcome ceremony for these girls and women was a joyful and enthusiastic worship of redeemed souls. These former slaves understood the power and the freedom of redemption in a way I never could. Their praise and adoration of the one true God was given with no inhibition whatsoever. It was refreshing and convicting all at the same time.

---

* For more information, see *International Needs* on page 117

Each day we went out to various villages to see a new school or church, to meet with the people of the villages who have benefited from this ministry.

One day we witnessed one of the negotiating sessions. We sat directly across from the head fetish priest of the village. Next to him sat his apprentice, a young man who appeared to be in his late teens or very early 20s. At the end of the negotiation, we approached the village leaders, which included the apprentice. As I moved close enough to see into the eyes of that young man, God filled my heart with forgiveness, love, and mercy. It was as if I could hear him say, "I am broken, I am in bondage, I am lost. I have no hope." God immediately brought to my mind the deep desperation of another broken soul: my daughter's rapist. God used this enounter, to clear my weed-infested heart. He enabled me to view these lost young men—both the priest's apprentice and my daughter's rapist—with compassion instead of judgment, forgiveness rather than bitterness.

> *God used this encounter, to clear my weed-infested heart.*

But there was still one more person I needed to forgive… Bethany. It was one thing to take the choke hold off the elusive someone who I was sure was lost and in bondage. It was another to recognize that my daughter's choice to leave us had left deep wounds of pain, shame, and resentment. If forgiving *him* meant having to go halfway around the world, forgiving *her* would mean going to a deep place within myself and facing the anger I held toward her.

Suicide is a cold, hard accusation that often communicates you weren't good enough, didn't help enough, didn't love enough. I understand it's not necessarily the intended message, but for those of us left as survivors, that's often how we feel. We just weren't *enough* for them.

I knew Bethany's actions weren't about me, but that's not how I felt. Besides the feelings of being "less than," and "not enough," there was still the pain of loss, the unmet expectations of life without her, and the mess she left behind. There were days I would go into her room, close the door, and let her have it. I was angry … at her. How could she do this … to me?

Mechanics or Mercy?

Matthew 18 records a question from Peter and a parable from Jesus. The question reveals a heart in search of a technicality, a way of limiting forgiveness. The parable teaches about mercy, unlimited forgiveness. (See Matthew 18:21-35.)

Those who know Christ have experienced the mercy of God. They know that God has cancelled their debt and will never seek to collect or punish. When we are unwilling to forgive, we are essentially sitting outside our prisoner's cell door waiting for restitution for which he has no means to pay. I submit that we are, therefore, in as much bondage as he.

✦ ✦ ✦

There's no way Bethany could ever undo or change her actions or the resulting ramifications. Neither could the man who raped her, for that matter. What made this grievance so particularly hard to forgive was the permanence of it. Certainly, I could see that not forgiving her held no consequence to her; I would be the only one serving time. Consequently, I could choose to sit on this side of an empty jail cell, essentially incarcerating myself as prison guard, or I could walk in freedom—freedom because of mercy extended to me by my Father and freedom due to my release of demands.

In *A Grace Disguised*, author Jerry Sittser writes, "Remembering the wrong done can make us a prisoner to pain and hatred, or it can make us the recipient of the grace, love, and healing power of God." We can focus on "the memory of a painful event that stands alone" or "the memory of a wonderful story. It can function as a catalyst that pushes us in a new direction, ... ”[2] For me, that new direction meant moving away from the prison cell.

At some point in this process we may be tempted to turn the blame, anger, or pain toward someone else entirely. Dare I say this? ... Sometimes we even try to put God in prison. Do we forgive God? Has He wronged us? Forgiveness assumes a wrong done. Since God is incapable of wrong, the answer to these questions is a resounding No! However, we still sometimes bind Him up as if He were to blame.

Or do we, rather, bind ourselves up, stifling our own walk with Him as a result?

We do not *forgive* God. We bow to Him in humility, acknowledging His sovereignty. His will is sometimes hard to understand, especially when we seek an answer through the lens of our pain. “To live with the sacred God of creation means that we conduct our lives with a God who does not explain Himself to us. It means that we worship a God who is often mysterious ... It means that God is not our best friend, our secret lover, or our good luck charm. He is God.”[3]

> *We do not forgive God. We bow to Him in humility, acknowledging His sovereignty.*

✦ ✦ ✦

I will continue in my lifetime to have opportunity to extend forgiveness for wrongs both great and small. I will have to wrestle with forgiving Bethany from time to time, I'm sure. Forgiveness is a process. I will continue to grow in this act of extending mercy. The longer I fix my eyes on God, the more I see how much I have been forgiven, and the more willing I am to offer mercy to others.

As I seek to honor my God by bowing to His will in my life through forgiveness and acceptance, I begin to grow toward a place of gratitude—even for my heartache. This is where the healing process begins, and I am able to see beauty in life once again. Slowly I emerge from the darkness of my own prison of grief into the light of His love. ✍

*Since parenting is hard,
I believe we would serve
one another well by
assuming the posture of
both humility and grace.*

❧ 10 ❧

LEAVING THE
LABELS BEHIND

O ur culture is obsessed with labels. If you don't own, wear, or have the right ones, you risk being ostracized by your peers. Parenting is no exception. We are particularly fond of labeling parents—what they do, what they don't do, how they do it. You get the picture.

Why am I jumping into the subject of parenting, you may wonder? Because I'm a mom whose daughter died by suicide, and I wrestle with the label that some have stamped onto my parenting skills as a result.

The Stigma of Suicide

When Bethany died, there was still a popular assumption—both in the culture at large and in the church—that only troubled teenagers from troubled homes took their own lives. She was the third teenager in our school district to die by suicide in four months' time. So naturally, when an article on the topic of teenage suicide appeared in the local newspaper a few months after she died, it caught my attention.

I was not prepared for what I read. The writer attempted to shed some light on the epidemic facing our little town, but he did so by lumping all three of the suicides together and basically blasting our families. He tried to show some respect by not mentioning names, but the dates and genders printed left no questions. He never called to offer condolences. He never called to interview us or request permission to write about our children or grieving families. He simply slapped a label on us. I cannot speak for the other families, but in our case, he didn't even come close to describing our family or her particular set of circumstances.

This reporter, as well as the editor who chose to run the story, were actually in line with the typical assumptions of the day. A stigma is often attached to the families of those who die by their own hand, although I'm not certain why. What have we done to deserve the hushed judgments, the whispers of the "how" surrounding their deaths? We are already overwhelmed with grief and are often more perplexed than anyone by our loved one's decision.

Yet, if I'm honest, we sometimes apply the label with our own hands. We take it upon ourselves, wear it, and suffer the shame. And you don't have to lose a child to suicide to understand what I'm talking about. All parents can be hard on themselves, too hard.

Parenting is challenging, perhaps one of the most difficult jobs on earth. Ironically, it is equally rewarding and filled with joyful experiences. It's certainly not a job for the faint of heart.

When you're already prone to performance mode as I am, insecurity and pride often take center stage, causing you to crave an ovation from family and friends. But the world is our critic, and everyone has an opinion they are more than happy to share. When we throw in the comparison game that plays out almost constantly through social media, we can easily overload on anxiety as we see the online successes of others held up against our own offline realities. The temptation to put a "not as" label onto ourselves or our children becomes overwhelming—not as pretty, not as intelligent, not as creative, not as . . .

A Parenting Manual, Please!

Parenting within the church can be especially challenging. The expectations placed on us are high and often unreasonable, no matter what life stage we're in—whether raising toddlers, teenagers, or even adults. As a result, we do our best to keep it under wraps when our children struggle. (Confession: This is for the parents' sake as much as it is for the children's.) We want to give the appearance of having it all together.

As parents, we have been entrusted with the bodies, souls, and minds of other human beings who have been created to think, feel, and make decisions for themselves. We have the responsibility to steer their natural desires and inclinations toward God, allowing these little ones to uniquely develop the way He designed them. Sounds simple, right? Yet, I have a hard enough time steering my own natural desires toward God. If you factor in the instruction of Scripture, the influences of culture, the ebb and flow of society's prejudices, unsolicited advice from sweet sister Grace at church, the glances and glares from other parents in your play group, and your own sleep deprivation, what do you have? Not simplicity, that's for sure.

It makes no difference to anyone that this child of yours is wired completely different from you, or has her own set of physical or mental battles to deal with. In fact, you seem to have little in common other than possibly your DNA. You simply cannot figure out what makes them tick.

And so I repeat, parenting is hard.

I thank God for the families whose children are capable young adults, living for the glory of Jesus Christ. I thank God especially for those families that we parented alongside when our children were little. Many of them are now enjoying their children as adults who are leading healthy, happy, and faithful lives. When our children were all little and we were walking the parenting journey together, we did mostly the same things parenting-wise. So, what made the difference? I'm not really sure, but I do know we all have unique products to work with.

As parents, we have no higher calling than to shepherd our children well, so we need to take the responsibility seriously and utilize the many tools and resources available to us. But we also need to remember that we are parenting little humans who have their own wills, who one day will grow up to be big humans that make their own decisions. We have the responsibility to control our parenting, but we have no guarantees of the results.

Proverbs 22:6 says, "Train up a child in the way he should go, and when he is old he will not depart from it." Many Christian parents have used this verse to beat themselves up. The problem with using a verse like this to hold one's self under the judgment of failure is that it was never intended to be a rule or a promise. The book of Proverbs is a book of wisdom poetry giving us principles of living that are generally true, not hard and fast promises. So, sound counsel and biblical wisdom for parenting? Yes. A court assessment for punishing sub-par parenting? No.

Since parenting is hard, I believe we would serve one another well by assuming the posture of both humility and grace. It is a humble-hearted parent who can truly put the needs of her children before her own, who accepts instruction, correction, and encouragement with grace. It is a humble-hearted parent who does not shape his own value upon the victories or the failures of his children. It is a humble-hearted parent who rejoices and who weeps with other parents and never stoops to compare. Because of the beautiful way humility and grace divinely coexist, the humble-hearted parent is also the grace-filled parent. This parent walks in humility while also coming alongside other moms and dads to encourage, support, pray for, and help. Truly, we are all in this together.

✦ ✦ ✦

I am grateful that the stigma once so heavily associated with suicide is fading, as much research has been done over the past couple of decades. Unfortunately, the problem of suicide itself has not. But I still find myself picking up that ill-fitted label from time to time. In counseling terms, being a survivor of a loved one who took their own life is categorized as "complicated grief." And it is complicated, as well as confusing. The act is so final that even if (as in Bethany's case) you have a reasonable amount of evidence as to the origin of the pain, you never have all your questions answered.

Because of the confusion, the shame, the unanswered questions, and all that the label brings with it, I am often reluctant to accept invitations to advise or share with parents. I'm tempted to believe that I have nothing to offer since it did not end well with one of my children. But this thinking is erroneous. It's a mindset that comes from taking my eyes off the grace of God—the very grace I have the opportunity to extend to other hurting parents. I have found that when I am willing to throw off any sort of self-applied label, I am able to see that God can use all of me—my victories, my failures, my joys, as well as my heartaches—to offer guidance, hope, or encouragement to others.

Our enemy would have us focus on our shortcomings as parents, keeping us distracted, defeated, and paralyzed, unable to accomplish this good work. He wants us to wear labels that divide, pulling us away from community that could infuse us with courage and strength as we take on this monumental task.

As Christian parents, we are commanded to walk out our lives, every aspect of them—including parenting—under the authority and guidance of the Holy Spirit. This encouraging command couples God's gift of the Spirit with our responsibility to submit to His leadership. This isn't a guarantee that our lives will be perfect and that our children will never hurt us, but we can walk in the freedom of obedience and leave the results to God alone.

Bob and I are connected to a church body that "does grace" well. Long before we became members, this group of believers carried one of their former pastor's family through the loss of their son to suicide. On top of that, our community group recognizes our need for prayer and encouragement—not only for us, but for everyone in the group. (We are all parents of adult children.) There is an atmosphere of transparency as most of us have at least one child who is wrestling with the world. This is good. It's as it should be, because parenting is hard, no matter what age our children are.

As we parent, let us walk in humility and extend grace. Let's leave behind the labels, and let us pray for one another in this very difficult but very beautiful journey. Let us love one another so well that none of us feel compelled to put ourselves under the strain of judgment.

✦ ✦ ✦

"So speak encouraging words to one another. Build up hope so you'll all be together in this, no one left out, no one left behind." (1 Thessalonians 5:11; *The Message*) ॐ

≈ 11 ≈

THE DIRT IN MY BROKEN HEART

I have been a Christ follower for over forty years. My life had been characterized by a consistent and deepening walk with Him. Somewhere down the road, though, my consistency turned into a charade. I had been redeemed, but I was in desperate need of renewal and restoration.

God began that work in my heart with Bethany's first visit to the emergency room. That night I caught a glimpse of the dirt in my heart—my pride, perfectionism, and fight for control. True reformation began then and there as God led me into a storm that would stir up the dirt and begin to cultivate it into rich soil. This meant a slow surrender of things I demanded, things I thought essential—reputation, the "Midas touch," perfect children, and a ministry free of stain or blemish. My offerings to God were rooted in performance and judgment, a striving to measure up. Obviously, I did not have an accurate assessment of grace and mercy, or of my own

> *True reformation began then and there as God led me into a storm that would stir up the dirt and begin to cultivate it into rich soil.*

desperation. Nor did I clearly understand the great transfer that happened on my behalf when Christ first rescued me. No more dirt, no more shame, no more striving. Instead, the opportunity for a garden of praise, beauty blooming out of gratitude.

> *"The funeral at which real life*
> *begins for each of us is the burying*
> *of one's own pride and self-sufficiency."* [1]
> (Ravi Zacharias, *Jesus Among Secular Gods*, pg. 177)

My daddy died while I was a college student. Although I was in anguish and I missed him terribly, I weathered that storm with my faith intact. Somewhere along the way, though, I was duped into thinking that I had done my share of suffering and that the future God had for me would be smooth sailing. After all, He owed that to me since I had gone through my trial so faithfully. I'm not sure where I got that idea, but it grew into an inclination toward pride. I began living my life in my own strength, continually offering my "goodness" to God. Looking back—it shames me to say this—my reason for not trusting God was because I felt He had wired me to do a great job on my own. That's what pride does. It deludes us into thinking that we are more capable than anyone else, even God.

That first night in the emergency room so many years ago sent my heart to the wrestling mat. In the middle of the reality that my daughter was fighting for her life, God confronted me with a choice that would ultimately save me: keep my perception of a perfect home or collapse into His capable care. Being perfect is exhausting and I was tired. God knew I desperately needed saving from myself, from my pride. In the shelter of this storm He would force me to begin to rest in Him, unveiling the end of me, my strength, and my own understanding. Each day would be a new decision to surrender, each step a new opportunity to choose Him.

Created to Choose

God created us to choose. It is this very thing that gave Eve the freedom to listen to the serpent and make a choice concerning her obedience to God, as well as Adam's opportunity to lead his wife in the way of righteousness or decide to follow in satisfying a destructive desire. It is the thing that gave Joseph the determination to do what was right instead of giving in to Potiphar's wife. Remember David? The Psalms are a reflection of his heart, crying out to God in his times of despair and fear. He was relentless in his assessment of circumstances, but consistent in choosing to defer to God's plan. He did, however, decide one day that he absolutely had to have Bathsheba to satiate a fire within himself. Later, he would choose to invite God in to examine and inspect his heart, opening himself to transformation.

Think about the ramifications of a people created just to obey a command: they would be nothing more than robots. Where's the glory in that? Or, what about a people who live in fear of a system of man-made impositions in order to gain the approval of their god? Instead we have a Holy Creator who put in us the ability to choose to whom we will be devoted. He also created our hearts to desire Him. The battle would forever be our striving to satisfy that longing with lesser things. Lovingly, He also provided a way to be wholly and forever deemed right in His eyes, ours for the choosing. The people who willingly decide to trust and obey are the ones who truly glorify their Maker. That's how God wants to receive glory, by seeing His creation *choose* Him. There is mystery to this choice, though. For even the choice is a gift from God, His Spirit drawing our spirit to Him. How beautiful is that? Someday, "At the name of Jesus *every knee* will bow, of those who are in heaven and on earth and under the earth, and that every tongue will confess that Jesus Christ is Lord, to the glory of God the Father" (Philippians 2:10-11, emphasis mine). But here and now, we have the opportunity to choose: Will we trust God in our circumstances or not?

Digging in the Dirt

In our lifetime, whether we realize it or not, our hearts are being cultivated, mostly by the sum of our experiences. We can keep the stony ground of our heart undisturbed, or we can allow ourselves to be influenced by God's love, and cultivate rich, fertile soil prepared for growth. Suffering exposes the kind of dirt we have cultivated. And in the aftermath of our trial, we are given a handful of seeds from which to choose. Some will sow seeds of despair, destruction, anger, and bitterness. Some will sow seeds of hope, determination, and compassion. Choosing to sow seeds of beauty is never more difficult than when we are suffering. In all of the pain, loss, and disappointment we will face in our lifetimes, we kneel in our private gardens and make choices as to which seeds we will sow in response to life.

> *Choosing to sow seeds of beauty is never more difficult than when we are suffering.*
>
>

Bethany made choices. I cannot chalk them up to her pain or excuse them away. Mental illness and trauma drive people to do things their loved ones don't understand. I held out hope that on the other side of her trauma Bethany would have a beautiful and incredible ministry to hurting girls and women. I didn't just hope, I was convinced it would be. That's who she was. She had always looked out for the underdog. She befriended the marginalized, the classmates that sat alone in the lunch room. She didn't like to see anyone alone or hurting. That's why I knew what she'd do with her life after this experience. But it's a strange thing, this power of choice—we can't choose for others.

When our children are young, we believe we can control what they do, and to a degree, we do. We make *some* choices for them and have a modicum of control: what they will wear, or what they'll eat for supper. But what about that meltdown they had in Aisle 3 today? Did mom choose *that* for them? What about the selfish heart that makes everything about him? Did dad choose *that* for his toddler? There's a name for this. It happened with the first choice—the one in the Garden that involved a tree and a serpent.

We Decide

We've become accustomed to softening this affront to our Creator. We've labeled it and re-labeled, but it really boils down to ... sin. We have a daily choice to make as to how we will respond to its prevalence in our hearts. We can choose differently.

There is this idea I call the "law of transfer" that says: if I wish or hope or influence enough on behalf of another, then they will make the choice I want them to make. But, in the garden of our hearts, there is no such law. The tilling of the soil there happens through many means and many hands, by way of life's experiences. However, only we ourselves have the power to decide which seeds will go in the soil. This truth dawned on me one morning as I was speaking to a group of women before Bethany's death. I was sharing her struggle and how it was affecting our family. I had shared the confidence I had for her amazing ministry I was sure she'd have someday. And then I heard it—the sound of the Holy Spirit, gently preparing and tilling the dirt in my heart. He spoke to me: "What if *her* choice is not *your* hope?"

> *Her choice might not be my hope, but His hope could be my choice.*

At that moment I realized that I could not keep Bethany from making the decisions she would make. I could pray, be involved, influence, support, help, direct, watch, but she had to make the choice to live through this or die. At the same time, *I* had a choice to make of my own. How would I respond? Suddenly, I realized that her choice might not be my hope, but His hope could be my choice.

Sometimes I sit down in a puddle of melancholy and ponder the what-ifs of life. What if that man had decided to have a tryst with a consenting woman on that ship instead of preying on a girl such as my young daughter? What if my daughter had chosen to tap into the resources of her faith, family, and friends for support instead of turning to anything she could get her hands on to dull the ache of her heart? What if we had never allowed her to go on that cruise in the first place? Dwelling on the what-ifs is essentially getting stuck in the mud. It's unproductive, a time waster, a procrastination of the decisions that ultimately need to be made. Slopping around in the mire of what if, or as John Bunyan so aptly put it, "the slough of despond," is just another way of denying the sovereignty of a loving, holy, and just God. At some point, we will have to dig in our dirt and make choices as to which seeds to plant. In our suffering, will we choose seeds of bitterness or joy? Critique or gratitude? Self-gratification or contentment? Demand for answers or faith?

Since we are human, oftentimes we have difficulty reconciling the truth of God's goodness to the evidence of what He allows. We have come to define "good" in a way that is often contrary to the facts of what we see happening in our lives or in the world around us. We have a difficult time seeing the "good" in tragedy and loss, in pain and suffering. We define God's character based upon what we can comprehend or understand; in essence, we are creating God in *our* image. That is dangerous. Do we really want our God to be limited by our finite way of thinking? Wouldn't He then cease to be God? Jen Wilkin reminds us, "Those who fear the Lord honor the limits he has placed on their minds, trusting what they do not, cannot or should not know to the One who does, perfectly."[2]

+ + +

Even if our response to grief yields a garden of praise, that growth does not always satisfy our longing to know why. If I could ask my daughter one thing, it would be, "Why? Why didn't you choose healing?" I suppose I ask God that, too, on occasion. I know so many women who lived the trauma Bethany did, and yet they chose life. The women I met in Africa had no support, no encouragement in their circumstances, and yet many of them are leading productive lives today. My questions will not be answered in this life, nor do I really need them to be. I have learned that perhaps the greater miracle—than having things turn out the way I wanted—was God's work in my heart when my circumstances weren't what I had hoped. I am not the miracle, God's work in me is. He has given me a choice, and He has given me the gift of choosing Him, however painful it has been.

Transparency and Faith

When we look through Scripture, we see myriad examples of God's people going through trials of various kinds. A common thread I see is a highlight of these sufferers being "real" with God. In their suffering, they are focused on God, they ask questions, they doubt, they struggle, but they recognize who God is and learn His character as He reveals it to them. I would like to suggest that when we go through trials and pain, that's when God does His soul-changing work in us. It is through this process that we become truer image-bearers of Him. We were created to reflect His image and His glory to the hopeless world around us.

We have the choice to move *through* or to just simply move *on* from our pain. What's the difference? Moving through acknowledges the hurt, asks the hard questions, and gives us a deeper understanding of the heart and character of God. It propels us forward into deeper intimacy with God and others. Moving on may allow for productivity, but it stifles true growth. It resigns us to our circumstances.

Healing, moving through, first takes us to the depth of our pain where we beg God for answers. It's a place where we truly meet God. It is in this dark place where we become weak and vulnerable and where God can begin His great work of revealing our need of Him and His strength. This process is not accomplished quickly. But as we surrender, we are able to hear Him, to see His perspective, to trust Him enough to see His better way. Our focus turns to Jesus and we fix our eyes on Him instead of our pain.

> *In choosing to merely move on, we forego the beauty of experiencing Him.*

This work of the heart will enable true healing to commence. As we rise from that deep place, we become more open to looking at how we can glorify God in our pain, and how God can use us to offer comfort to others. We may occasionally be swept up in our grief, because it will never be fully removed until the "better" comes, but we will have deeper peace.

Moving on, however, never yields visible healing, the desire to actually begin again. We stuff, we resolve, we tap into the strength of our natural man, limited as it is, and we move on. But our hearts are just a little bit calloused, our minds a tad cynical. We may continue the outward motion of our quest for God, but only as it pertains to knowledge, for there is no desire for true intimacy with Him. In choosing to merely move on, we forego the beauty of experiencing Him. In our brokenness we push away the blessing in order to protect our hearts. We never fully enter in to "the fellowship of His sufferings" (Philippians 3:10). Accepting the pain without the experience of wrestling with it never yields anything beautiful. Eventually our acceptance turns into resignation, which turns into bitterness. The bitterness can stay hidden for a long time, like a root deeply buried, but it will eventually surface.

God in His awesome power has the ability to change our circumstances and answer our prayers the way we want Him to—and often He does—but it is also good of Him to desire us to be drawn closer into Him as we learn to trust Him and see Him for who He is. In our pain, *through* our loss, will we allow Him to deepen our roots of faith?

Have I finally conquered my formidable foes of pride or perfectionism? Not by a long shot. I am aware of their presence almost daily. However, I am also much more aware of my need for God. As I wrestle with the pride that so easily walks into my heart, I must fight it with truth, facing it head on as I surrender my thoughts to God. I must remind myself of what is actually true and acknowledge where I am exalting myself. By way of example, releasing this book into the world has revealed to me that my desire for perfection still exists. Perhaps the struggle in writing was not necessarily reliving these events, for I am walking in the healing power of God, but rather deciding what to include, how to say it, the ever-present "What will they think?" buried deep in my heart. But this—confessing these thoughts to you and to God—battles the enemy.

> *He loved me enough to carry me through heartache so I could see that I needed Him to carry me through life itself.*

That night so many years ago God began to rescue me from thinking I could survive this life by relying on my own resources. He began to pull down the façade of perfectionism. He loved me enough to carry me through heartache so I could see that I needed Him to carry me through life itself. He gently placed me down in soil He had prepared and offered me the life-giving opportunity to plant a garden of glory, pointing always and only to His goodness. ❧

*God energizes our hope
when we extend to others
the comfort we have
received from Him.*

❧12❧

HOPE

Many of us belong to a club we didn't willingly join—the divorcee club, the depression club, the widowed club... I belong to the grief club.

I was eighteen when my daddy died. He was my world. I expected his death—he had been sick for a long time—but I wasn't prepared for the pain that would come after losing him. Even so, as a young believer, I was able to hold on to my trust in God. I believe my faith was a gift from God because loss so often unsettles our core beliefs.

Through the subsequent losses in my life, I have persevered in my faith, though not without wrestling or occasionally shaking my fist at Him in resentment. There have been times when I would rather have plopped down and wallowed in my own sadness than to walk alongside someone else in theirs. But I've learned that God energizes our hope when we extend to others the comfort we have received from Him.* In such times, God reminds me that Jesus willingly suffered and gave His life for me. He took on the sorrow and heartache of this life, in order to offer me hope.

✦ ✦ ✦

---

* 2 Corinthians 1:4 (paraphrased)

As I write this final chapter, we are coming upon the fifteenth anniversary of Bethany's death—fifteen long years since I've held her and looked into her beautiful face. She'd be thirty-one.

I sometimes wonder how life would have turned out for her if she had never stepped foot on that cruise ship. Would she be married? Have a family? Would Bob and I be enjoying curly-haired grandbabies?

I think it's okay to wonder every once in a while. This is what the Bible calls "hope deferred" (Proverbs 13:12). But it's not okay for me to dwell there. I can consider the what-could-have-been times had Bethany lived, but I cannot linger long over them. That point of view gives me no hope. And I need hope.

The hope we find in Christ doesn't magically change our circumstances, but it does bring a new and better perspective. Given the rise of anxiety and anger in our world and the personal pain that we all encounter in life, it is vital to understand what real hope is, and more importantly, to know the only reliable source of hope.

The Dictionary and the Bible

Perhaps it is cliché to introduce a topic with, "According to the dictionary, such and such means..." So, please allow me to be trite for a moment.

The dictionary generally defines *hope* in two ways: (1) a feeling of expectation and desire for a certain thing to happen, and (2) a feeling of trust. The second definition is considered archaic, which is too bad because it is actually closer to the biblical meaning. In lessening—perhaps even losing—this definition of hope we have lost much of the difference that hope can make in our lives. Hope built on trust is much more life-giving than hope that is made up of wishes and desires, especially when that trust is placed in God.

What I find most interesting about the Bible's description of hope is how it is introduced in the Old Testament and fulfilled in the New. Over a dozen Hebrew words are translated into the English word *hope* in the Old Testament, presenting God as a refuge and help. In contrast, the New Testament, which for the most part was originally written in Greek, has only two forms of one word that is translated *hope*. The word essentially merges the ideas of hope from the Old Testament into one, and means "to anticipate, or to desire something good with the expectation of obtaining it."[1]

The Jewish people had great hope; they had been living with the expectation of their promised Messiah for hundreds of years. So, when Jesus entered the scene and said, "Do not think that I came to abolish the Law or the Prophets; I did not come to abolish but to fulfill" (Matthew 5:17), He proclaimed that He was the long-anticipated fulfillment of their hope. As the promised One, and the perfect One, He could secure for them a permanent relationship with God. He could transform their hope from expectation to assurance. This is why the apostle Paul could later write, "We exult in hope of the glory of God … and hope does not disappoint" (Romans 5:2, 5). Jesus was—and is—the hope.

He could transform their hope from expectation to assurance.

In that same passage, Paul mentions something else in which we can rejoice: our tribulations. That's a strange thing to rejoice in, isn't it? Yet the book of James says the same thing: "Consider it all joy, my brethren, when you encounter various trials" (James 1:2). There's a beautiful progression that takes place when we allow God to do His work through our trials—"Tribulation brings about perseverance; and perseverance, proven character; and proven character, hope; and hope does not disappoint" (Romans 5:3-5). In God's hands, our heartaches move our hope from desire and expectation into confidence and completion.

Could it be that the only way to cultivate a heart fully surrendered to Him is by walking through a valley and enduring pain? That the only way to truly radiate Jesus Christ is by carrying a very small part of what He suffered while on this earth?

Moving Forward

Hope directs us toward the future, it propels us forward and keeps us going. I think that's why Paul tells us to rejoice in it, because if we have hope, we are still moving forward. The opposite is also true: if we are hope-less we are focused on the past and losing ground. We should remember, learn from, and even be grateful for our past, but only in ways that will help us in what lies ahead.

The book of Hebrews is known for how deeply it speaks to the subject of faith, but it also has much to say about hope. In many ways, the two are similar. They are both needed on earth but will no longer be needed in Heaven because they will have been fulfilled by the very presence of Jesus Christ.

But for now, we need them. We desperately need them. And what good would our faith be if it didn't have any hope attached? To a hurting world that may be wondering what we have to offer, shouldn't our profession of faith and our confession of hope look pretty much the same? If we profess to have faith but trudge through our pain without the slightest evidence of hope, what good would our faith be? Really, I think that the hope I possess *is* the proof of my faith, the means by which others can see Jesus Christ. I endure and persevere—with joy—and the world encounters Him.

After the Fact

In the story of Mary, Martha, and Lazarus, recorded in John 11, Jesus comes onto the scene *after* Lazarus has died. He reveals Himself to Martha as "the resurrection and the life." Was this a statement of a pending miracle, or was Jesus pointing to something even greater? Humanly speaking, we know Jesus can intervene before death, but the significance of the resurrection is that He is able to help *after* death. It is, in fact, the triumph over death, the victory over the grave that has secured our hope for eternity. Lazarus is raised only to eventually die again. Obviously. My daughter is still dead. That's life here on earth. But my hope lies beyond this life, and even beyond death—all the way into eternity. Jesus Christ is the source of life and the fulfillment of hope.

My confidence is not that I might one day be reunited with those who've gone before me, though that thought gives me joy. I'm not exactly sure how our past relationships will look in heaven. Bethany was a good gift here, as were my parents and other friends who have passed. We were created to enjoy community, but we will always experience loss as long as we are dealing with earthbound relationships, because all people die. Please don't take this as an argument for isolating ourselves from others to avoid the pain of grief. Rather, let it point you to the single relationship in life that will never fade away—with God through His Son, Jesus Christ. Christ is our confident security because He is eternal. This relationship will not end. We cannot lose Christ.

This hope has altered my perspective on life, not only for the future, but also for the here and now.

✦ ✦ ✦

Bethany died in her room. My living hope causes me to rejoice in the fact that one of my overnight guests accepted Christ as her Savior in that very room. Death was shattered by hope—in a place that once housed chaos. Four walls and some pretty decorations to most, but to me, it is now the space where a miracle took place.

Our experience has given us unique opportunity to offer comfort to those suffering the loss of a child from suicide. On one particular occasion, we were called upon to visit an acquaintance in her loss. I walked up to this grieving mother, shook her hand

and said, "We know what you're going through." Her eyes glazed over from yet another platitude. Noticing this, I continued, "No, we do … we are Bethany's parents." With that her eyes quickened as if to say, "You Do!" Because of our loss, we were in a position to extend heartfelt understanding and hope.

I could recount many other times when God has shown Himself real to us all over again because we were witness to His work around us, even *through* us. And hope enables us to see God at work even in the small things. When I look for God in the everyday joys of life, choosing to attribute those things to His hand, my awareness of His presence and work in my life increases. Then, when the not-so-pleasant realities of life take place, my heart is conditioned to know that He is there even then.

✦ ✦ ✦

Hope calls us to a better perspective, an eternal one that transcends our temporary circumstances. Because of Christ, I can press on when I want to give up, curl up, and shrivel up. When I can no longer stand in my pain, I can collapse into His arms until I am restored to stand again. The hope I have is not something I expect to be completed on this side of heaven; it beckons me to something better. I can't give it to you, but it can be yours by trusting Christ and His work on your behalf. He alone can awaken your soul to new life, resulting in new hope.

> *When I can no longer stand in my pain, I can collapse into His arms until I am restored to stand again.*
>
>

The God I've been speaking about throughout this book is not a "higher being" subject to our whims or desires. He is God—the Almighty One.

I am in awe that He would seek me out and has promised to hold my hand as I walk through this valley. What other god sees our pain, knows what we need, and loves us enough to be with us? Most of the things that crowd out the one true God in my life never offer any comfort or hope, much less stick around to walk beside me. Those things only take. They demand my time, my attention, as well as my resources. They never give in return.

Walking in Confidence

The expectations of life with my daughter are gone—a wedding, grandchildren, adult friendship. In their place are sweet memories and gratitude for having been part of her life. I'm learning to not take loss so personally. I weep, I hurt, I wrestle, but I also recognize pain is part of living in a broken world. My expectation has shifted from the uncertainty of life's relationships to a confident security in my relationship with Christ. As I walked in my pain shortly after her death, I came to a crossroad. A decision had to be made. Would I choose despair, brokenness, and bitterness, or would I choose hope? Psalm 73:28 states, "But as for me, the nearness of my God is good; I have made the Lord God my refuge, that I may tell of all your works."

Through loss, God graciously exposed the pride in my heart that manifested as a deep-seated need to please, perform, and be perfect. It affected my parenting and relationships, as well as my personal time with God, my identity, and my service. As I grew in my understanding of the character and heart of God through study and prayer, I grew increasingly amazed at His holiness and His character, and also His deep love for me. This led to authentic worship, praise, and service. I was able to be honest with God about my disappointments and loss, and I trusted him to lead me to a place of healing. Now, I walk in confidence knowing I can trust Him and can relinquish my story into His capable hands to use for His glory, however He chooses.

✦ ✦ ✦

So here we are at the end of this book, but by no means the end of my story. I've given you a peek into my broken heart and the dirt God has revealed through my time in the valley. He is still cultivating. The loss of my precious daughter is not and will not be my only test of faith in this life. I know it. There have already been other tests. So, the dirt continues to be tilled. God is so faithful, He is good, and He continues to show His love, His forgiveness, and His care for me.

✦ ✦ ✦

I wrote this book for two reasons. The first is simply because God asked me to write it. So, in obedience, I wrote. The second reason is you. You may have walked in a valley as well and you may be second-guessing the goodness of God. Whoever you are and whatever your reason for reading through to the end, my prayer, my hope, my desire is for you to be able to have complete confidence in God. I want you to see God in His splendor. I want you to have hope.

Hope doesn't take away pain. Hope doesn't fix situations. Hope gives rest to your heart and soul. Hope allows you to deeply trust, to know that God is good, that He has a plan for this world, and that he has invited you and me to participate in it. I want you to know beyond a shadow of a doubt that you are loved, you are forgiven, and you are deeply cared for. This confidence results in nothing but rest for you and glory for Him.

> *Blessed be the God and Father of our Lord Jesus Christ, who according to His great mercy has caused us to be born again to a living hope through the resurrection of Jesus Christ from the dead, to obtain an inheritance which is imperishable and undefiled and will not fade away, reserved in heaven for you, who are protected by the power of God through faith for a salvation ready to be revealed in the last time. In this you greatly rejoice, even though now for a little while, if necessary, you have been distressed by various trials, so that the proof of your faith, being more precious than gold which is perishable, even though tested by fire, may be found to result in praise and glory and honor at the revelation of Jesus Christ. (1 Peter 1:3-7)*

I have had a whole team of people who have been praying for a very long time for *you*. I have been praying for you too. Friend, your hope will never be found in your circumstances. Hope is *always* and *only* found in Jesus Christ. Don't fear the pain. Allow Him to lift the darkness and replace it with the light of hope, even in the midst of heartbreak. ⁊

Endnotes

Chapter 1: Truth Serum
[1] Amy E. Spiegel, *Letting Go of Perfect*, pg. 96
[2] C. J. Mahaney, Humility: *True Greatness*, pg. 138

Chapter 2: Making a Molehill Out of a Mountain
[1] From a sermon of Pastor J. Josh Smith

Chapter 3: Learning to Let Go
[1] Jen Wilkins, *None Like Him*, pg. 25

Chapter 6: Peace That Passes Understanding
[1] Ann Voskamp, *One Thousand Gifts*, pgs. 151-152
[2] C. J. Mahaney, *Humility: True Greatness*, pg. 141

Chapter 7: Cherish the Moment
[1] Jerry Sittser, *A Grace Disguised*, pgs. 176-77

Chapter 8: A Teacup Full of Memories
[1] Jerry Sittser, *A Grace Disguised*, pg. 66

Chapter 9: Forgiveness
[1] Charles Stanley, *The Gift of Forgiveness*, pg. 16
[2] Jerry Sittser, *A Grace Disguised*, pg. 146
[3] M. Craig Barnes, *When God Interrupts*, pg. 135

Chapter 11: The Dirt in My Broken Heart
[1] Ravi Zacharias, *Jesus Among Secular Gods,* pg. 177
[2] Jen Wilkins, *None Like Him*, pg. 119

Chapter 12: Hope
[1] *Complete Word Study, SZ*, pg. 570

Noted Ministries

~ Radiant Hope ~

"In 2016, my wife, Courtney, and I founded a non-profit called Radiant Hope. Through this work we seek to restore identity and dignity to those affected by injustice and create safe spaces where girls and women can flourish. While God gave this heart and vision to Courtney, it resonated with me because of my experience with Bethany. We operate in Eastern Romania, and our main focus is to spend quality time and build healthy relationships with girls in the government orphanages. These girls come from a wide variety of backgrounds, all of which are littered with trauma. As we seek to reduce their vulnerabilities and increase their opportunities, our anthem to them is the same message that I used to say to Bethany, 'You are loved, you are valued, and you are not defined by the injustices that you have faced in your life.'"

—RICKY BOLANDER, Bethany's brother

If you'd like to learn more about Radiant Hope,
please visit our website at **www.radianthope.org**.

~ International Needs ~

I am happy to report that since the initial writing of this book, the practice of Tricosi has been abolished in Ghana, West Africa. International Needs Ghana has been able to redirect its focus of the work there to resource, empowerment, and education.

"When you support the Center for Empowerment and Enterprise Development (CEED), you are investing in the future. As young people from around the country gather to learn skills that will help them run their own businesses, the Lord continues to use this ministry to transform entire communities." *(Taken from International Needs website)*

For more information on International Needs please visit their website at **https://internationalneeds.us/**.

ABOUT *the* AUTHOR

Alongside her pastor-husband, Bonnie walked through her daughter's rape and consequent suicide in 2003. She has experienced deep healing and growth through this trial, and considers it a great honor to be involved in the lives of women. Whether it is teaching, facilitating small groups, sharing her story at retreats, mentoring, hospitality, or training in life skills and organization, her joy is encouraging women in their walk with Christ and guiding them in the truth of His word.

Bonnie has a BA in Church Administration with a concentration in youth and music from Bob Jones University. She and her best friend, Bob, have been married since 1984. They have two sons and two lovely daughters-in-love. She and Bob served two different churches in Michigan for 17 years before moving to Texas. She currently serves at MacArthur Blvd. Baptist Church in Irving, TX in the choir, on the women's ministry team, leads women's Bible studies and teaches a weekly Bible class. She and her husband enjoy mentoring young engaged or married couples. She has taught many classes on Biblical Womanhood, was a mentor mom for MOPS, and has trained on life skills such as hospitality and organization. She has spoken at women's retreats, home based business retreats, and MOPS groups, and has been sharing their story for many years. Her desire is to point women to the truth of the character of God, encouraging them to trust God's hand and heart through their heartaches.

Bonnie enjoys traveling the world with her husband and is looking forward to having grandchildren this year. She finds great pleasure serving others in her home. She and her husband reside in Flower Mound, Texas.

For more information and to connect with Bonnie please vist www.BoundbyHope.com